"I can think of at least two good reasons for reading this delightful book. First, the leadership lessons that include the author's story are as engaging as they are compelling. A brilliant student who studied engineering while becoming fascinated by leadership at an early age, Shantha Mohan jumps off the page in a way that makes you wish she was a friend living nearby. Second, it's just plain fun to think about these old Beatles songs as leadership lessons."

Amy C. Edmondson, *Professor, Harvard Business School;*
Author of The Fearless Organization: Creating Psychological
Safety in the Workplace for Learning, Innovation, and Growth

"Leadership Lessons with The Beatles is an extraordinary literary tour de force and a worthy addition to the catalog of must-have actionable business books. Principally a guide to developing leadership skills, it uses the important themes of several famous Beatles songs to explore and teach the core skills that great leaders exhibit. But it's so much more than that. Shantha takes the reader on a journey through contemporary technology history, including many of her own personal stories and experiences, stopping to share the lessons of successful organizations and their leaders such as PepsiCo, Microsoft, Tesla, Starbucks, and many others. At each step, leadership tools and techniques are explained in simple and practical terms. Shantha has written an accessible and practical book for aspiring leaders, existing leaders, and anyone interested in developing important skills for the 21st century economy. Of course, fans of The Beatles, like myself, will get a particular kick from Shantha's approach to the subject matter."

Jonathan Reichental, *Founder, Professor, and Author*

"Just like music resonates deeply, striking a chord within us that moves and motivates, *Leadership Lessons with The Beatles* will resonate with everyone who desires to improve our world by investing in others. In the dynamic world, the need for outstanding leadership remains unchanged, and Shantha allows the reader to learn key lessons she discovered in her successful career. The powerful yet straightforward advice she offers will help others create an environment where people flourish, supporting employees to do their jobs and meet their own needs. Her guidance will help all of us become better leaders and better people."

Peter Boatwright, *Professor, Tepper School of Business; Director, Integrated Innovation Institute, Carnegie Mellon University*

"Shantha has a ticket to ride the wealth of experience garnered during a distinguished career as an entrepreneurial leader to deliver these pearls of wisdom. Full of down-to-earth common sense, this book is akin to a best friend giving much-needed heartfelt advice like a blackbird singing in the dead of night. In this post-COVID world, it heralds in a good day's sunshine. Imagine coming together to discuss any problem with a little help from your friends. Let it be part of your magical mystery tour of leadership."

Stuart Evans, *Distinguished Service Professor, Integrated Innovation Institute, Carnegie Mellon University Silicon Valley*

"After reading so many different books on leadership over the years, I sort of lost interest in the subject and hadn't read one in many years. Shantha's refreshing approach to the topic is brilliant, and it sucked me right in. I think I was in the third chapter before I realized I was still standing up and needed to find a comfortable place to sit and read the rest. Familiar metaphors are powerful tools for illustrating and learning new ideas. Shantha nails this in a powerful and entertaining way by tying in her own hard-earned and unique leadership lessons with our collective and near universal familiarity with different Beatles songs that bring each chapter to life. I've since dusted off my Beatles collection and have been putting Shantha's unique leadership lessons to work."

Mark Bowles, *Serial Entrepreneur*

"Leadership Lessons with The Beatles highlights sixteen ways to become a better leader, each featuring actionable tips and anchored in a well-known Beatles song. (My personal favorite? "All You Need Is Love!") Hear any of those songs and you can't help but be reminded of the book's great insights."

Alan Eagle, *Co-author of* How Google Works *and* Trillion Dollar Coach

"Shantha Mohan delivers insightful leadership advice to both novice and seasoned leaders, uniquely aligning her real-life examples with universally recognized story tellers. *Leadership Lessons with The Beatles* brings together multiple core concepts for elegant management success into a concise, engaging journey."

Dave McCandless, *Information Technology Executive, Advisor and Lecturer, current Senior Director Information Technology, Guardant Health*

"Have you ever pondered the possibilities of merging the unquenchable spirit and optimism of The Beatles' timeless music with a humanist-oriented business strategy? Shantha Mohan's *Leadership Lessons with The Beatles* does precisely that. In this way, Mohan gifts the world with a winning approach to affording our business lives with the Fab Four's unique balance of buoyancy and goodwill. Better yet, Mohan demonstrates the myriad ways in which a humanist outlook not only benefits the world of business, but can help it truly thrive."

Kenneth Womack, *Author of* John Lennon 1980:
The Last Days in the Life

"I was lucky to have Shantha as my mentor and role model early in my career. It is beautiful to see the standards she lived by transformed into leadership lessons in *Leadership Lessons with The Beatles*. The essays in the book will help you become a better leader—for example, "Within You Without You," on becoming a humble leader—and how to live life to the fullest. If you are an aspiring leader, use this book as your guide and inspiration."

David Sun, *CEO, SF Healthcare*

Leadership Lessons
with The Beatles

Leadership Lessons with The Beatles

Actionable Tips and Tools for Becoming Better at Leading

Shantha Mohan

Foreword by
Dr. Anand Deshpande,
Founder and Chairperson of Persistent Systems

Routledge
Taylor & Francis Group

A PRODUCTIVITY PRESS BOOK

First published 2022
by Routledge
605 Third Avenue, New York, NY 10158

and by Routledge
4 Park Square, Milton Park, Abingdon, Oxon, OX14 4RN

Routledge is an imprint of the Taylor & Francis Group, an informa business

© 2022 Shantha Mohan

ISBN: 9781032212586 (hbk)
ISBN: 9781032212562 (pbk)
ISBN: 9781003267546 (ebk)

DOI: 10.4324/9781003267546

Typeset in Garamond
by Deanta Global Publishing Services, Chennai, India

To Illyria

Contents

Foreword

It is an honor and a pleasure to write this foreword for Shantha Mohan's fascinating book *Leadership Lessons with The Beatles*.

Many of us who join companies as engineers start in technical roles and, over our careers, move into management and leadership roles. This transition is difficult and stressful, as we are not trained and prepared for this change. I started as a Member of Technical Staff at Hewlett-Packard Laboratories straight after my Ph.D. In my first job, I worked on databases for software engineering environments related to the work during my Ph.D. thesis. It was during this time I had the pleasure of meeting Shantha and V.J. Mohan. V.J. was my senior colleague at HP Labs, and Shantha worked at Consilium at the time. They lived close by, and I was a regular Sunday brunch visitor at their home.

After a short stint as a techie, I moved back to India to start Persistent. Besides the technical work, I was immediately responsible for administration, sales, and building and leading a team. I learned on the job. My father worked with me at Persistent, and I had a few friends who were running their own businesses. We experimented and learned from each other. The company was small, and I could make mistakes on the way. Over the years, as the company grew and new people joined the team, I saw the ambitious programmers struggle to transition to leadership and managerial positions. This transition to leadership roles is not easy. Good programming skills do not translate to leadership and people management skills. And this is where this book is a blessing.

I have participated both as a facilitator and as a participant in several "First-Time Manager" classes, but getting the right mix of techniques, stories, and experience in a short program is incredibly difficult. Shantha's book addresses this void.

I love the way the book is organized. Each chapter is unique and is entirely written from the point of view of the new leader. Each chapter, set on the theme of a Beatles song title, is independent and can be read individually and must be read repeatedly. Each chapter uses personal experience stories from Shantha's long and distinguished leadership career. She shares a set of well-accepted management principles and techniques that would help aspiring managers frame the problem and create a structure to articulate the problem. For example, in Chapter 1,"Getting Better," she describes the ABCDE method to build optimism in difficult situations. Besides describing the technique, Shantha shares personal examples and stories to illustrate the point and help aspiring managers put these techniques into practice.

As Shantha describes in her chapter on "The Long and Winding Road," the leadership journey is strenuous and is more akin to a marathon than a sprint. I have observed that aspiring managers are always trying to do too much. They have their hands full. Over the years, I have learnt the importance of prioritization, delegation, and empowering the team. These are hard things to do. Shantha does a great job of helping aspiring managers build the team's capabilities and create an environment to succeed.

The safety announcement on every flight, "put on your own oxygen mask first before you help others," is relevant in the leadership journey. Leaders must set an example. Like Mahatma Gandhi said, "Be the change you want to see in the world."

The leadership journey must start from "self." Shantha shares several tips that would help first-time managers to build skills and capabilities to set an example for their team members. All of us have many things to do, but those who prioritize better are more productive and effective. Prioritization requires discipline and training. There is always an impulse to chase the most recent interruption, but you can miss the big picture when you do that. I have found that maintaining a written task list and scheduling time for specific tasks helps me get things done. The feeling that work is not in control is highly stressful. Life feels much more in control when you have a clear list of things to work on and time allocated for the tasks.

Shantha discusses the importance of communication and the importance of negotiation and conflict resolution. Positive conflicts create energy in teams, while negative disputes can be draining. There is a fine line between the two, and it is the leader's responsibility to create an environment of active collaboration. I have followed four steps to building positive energy in teams. The first is mission. We all need a purpose, and it helps to get the team to come together to define a joint mission or purpose, which allows the team to focus. The second is alignment. It is essential to have the team aligned with our mission. Alignment works well when every team member knows their role and how their work aligns with the project's mission. The third is empowerment. Leaders must delegate and empower every single member to make decisions that are appropriate to their role. And, finally, trust. We all work best when we trust each other. The leader has a vital role to play in building confidence in the team, which starts with the leader trusting every member to do what is right! Being genuine and transparent is an essential first step. Shantha has some excellent tools for managing self and the team.

I found the chapter "Help!" on building a network of mentors and seeking help very thought-provoking. Leadership can be lonely, and having a network of mentors and supporters is crucial during tough times. You cannot build this network in a time of crisis. As they say, you cannot start digging a well when there is fire. I find developing a network of mentors and supporters is a very crucial skill for aspiring managers to acquire. Mentors are everywhere, and it is more about what we learn rather than what they teach.

I found the final chapter, "When I'm Sixty-Four," to be very compelling. Shantha asks some fundamental questions about work–life balance that I think about often, but I have always struggled to resolve. As I near the magic age of 64, my advice to an aspiring manager would be to involve everyone in the family to be part of your career plans and not feel sorry for yourself.

The references to Beatles music and stories give an exciting dimension to the book. I really enjoyed listening to The Beatles playlists as I read through the book.

I believe this book would be an excellent reference for all aspiring leaders. Follow through on the resources and try some of the "To Practice" ideas at the end of each chapter. Then, when you confront a situation, it would be worthwhile to reread the specific chapter!

With best wishes to all the aspiring leaders!

Anand Deshpande
Founder, Chairperson and Managing Director,
Persistent Systems

Acknowledgements

I owe this book to the music of The Beatles, which inspires me every day.

My longtime friend Anand Deshpande graciously agreed to look at a couple of my chapters in their rawest form and gave me precious input. I am forever in his debt for writing the foreword. He embodies what it is to be a humble leader who has the indomitable will to succeed. It is a great honor to have him talk about this book, and I am humbled.

It is hard to find the words to express my gratitude adequately to the brilliant and respected Amy Edmondson, Jonathan Reichental, Peter Boatwright, Stuart Evans, Mark Bowles, Alan Eagle, Dave McCandless, Kenneth Womack, and David Sun. I feel blessed to have their endorsements.

I am forever grateful to my friends from various disciplines: Pete Carey, Abhijeet Bhadra, Edward Dixon, Balaraman Jayaraman, Syed Khaleel Ahmed, Stephanie Charles, Sharmi Surianarain, Vanathi Sethupathi, and Karl Waldman. They were kind enough to review one or more early drafts, and their thoughtful reviews and suggestions made the writing so much better. Their encouragement and wise counsel were vital to this book, and thank you!

I am very thankful to the leaders who permitted me to use their quotes, writings, frameworks, and concepts; I stand on their shoulders.

My work at Consilium and Retail Solutions taught me many of my leadership lessons. I am thankful to my teams, colleagues, and the cofounders at Retail Solutions for their support when navigating my leadership tensions.

It is a privilege to be at my alma mater, Carnegie Mellon University, where I continue to practice my leadership skills, especially mentoring and lifelong learning.

My editor at Taylor & Francis, Kristine Mednansky, cheered me on from the proposal to the publication of this book. She guided me through the complex maze of getting permissions and answered all my questions when I had doubts.

Leandro Stavorengo designed the illustration for the cover of this book. Thank you, Leandro, for your creativity and bringing the theme alive.

Finally, I couldn't have written this book without the support of my family—my raison d'être.

About the Author

Dr. Shantha Mohan is a mentor and project guide at Carnegie Mellon University's Integrated Innovation Institute. She cofounded Retail Solutions Inc., a leader in retail data analytics, and ran its global product development organization. Her prior experiences include technical and educational consulting and running worldwide product development for Consilium, a Manufacturing Execution System company (acquired by Applied Materials). She graduated with a Ph.D. in Operations Management from the Tepper School of Management, Carnegie Mellon University, and has an undergraduate degree in Electronics & Communication from the College of Engineering, Guindy (CEG), India.

Shantha is passionate about equality, diversity, and sustainability and is a member of the Society of Women Engineers (SWE), where she is a volunteer and mentor. She is the author of *Roots and Wings: Inspiring Stories of Indian Women in Engineering* and a coauthor of *Demystifying AI for the Enterprise: A Playbook for Business Value and Digital Transformation*, published by Routledge Press. Shantha is a Distinguished Toastmaster (DTM), and she serves on the board of CEG alumni, North America (CEGAANA), and helped to create a student mentorship program and the CEG Betterment program.

Introduction

Something that has always resonated with me and fills me with fond memories is that somehow, no matter what, we always ended with mutual respect for the other's position. To me, that is precious and somewhat rare. Thank you for that. I always held your dedication, knowledge, ethics, and willingness to help in the highest regards—professionally and personally. I will miss all of that and want to thank you for the experience and pleasure of working with you as well as for the opportunity of getting to know you.

I hope when I grow up to be Shantha's age, I could be in the same state like her—always young, always learning new knowledge, always impacting others in the positive way.

When I retired from the company I cofounded (where I was the Chief Development Officer), sendoff messages[1] such as the above overwhelmed me with gratitude.

I did not always have the interpersonal skills to earn such praise.

It was the 1990s. I was a director of engineering. I sat down with my manager for my performance review. He handed me his evaluation, and I gave him my self-review. We spent the next several minutes in silence while we read the documents. Once I finished reading, I looked up and waited for my manager to start the conversation. My review and promotion didn't surprise me. The paragraph which talked about opportunities for improvements was the one on top of my mind. It said:

> *Patience—In past years Shantha was quick to show displeasure with those who did not meet her high standards, including herself. Shantha has made excellent progress in controlling her feelings but allows her frustration to get the better of her.*

We talked about it, and I asked him what I could do to rectify my shortcomings. He said the company was going to get me personal leadership training. The coach I worked with used a 360-degree assessment to put a plan together for my learning, and off I went on my executive leadership journey.

My love of leadership started when I was in elementary school. Every year, each class elected a student leader, and every year I was one. The leadership duties I carried out served the teacher and the students of the class. I represented the class in the student council. I cleaned the chalkboard. I kept the supplies stocked. I ran errands for the teacher, such as taking the attendance records to the school office. I didn't realize it, but I was practicing "servant leadership." This is a phrase coined by Robert K. Greenleaf in *The Servant as Leader.*[2]

After getting an engineering degree, I joined the Electronics Corporation of India (ECIL) as Technical Officer. I took a break from my career when I got married, had a child, and moved to the United States with my family. I continued my education after my child was able to go to preschool, got a Ph.D. in Operations Management from Carnegie Mellon University's Tepper Business School, and joined a company called Consilium. There, I grew from a software engineer to project lead, manager, and director. Eventually, I became the worldwide head of software development.

I enhanced my leadership skills by creating new teams, training them, and leading them to deliver new generations of software systems. As I progressed in my career, I also enhanced my skills in negotiation, empowering my teams and contributing to the company's strategy. I also learned about doing the right thing for the good of my team and the organization. Soon after, another company acquired us, and I had to lay off several of my team members in a cost-cutting measure. I put myself on the layoff list, sparing a few of my team members. They could continue sustaining the engineering efforts. Looking back, I am thankful that I was thinking for myself. I was not simply following what came down from the business head.

At Consilium, I worked with many Fortune 500 companies. Semiconductor industry leaders such as Intel, AMD, Siemens, and SGS-Thompson were my customers. They taught me everything about caring for customers. I had the opportunity to visit them around the world. I learned from a diverse group of people. When I left Consilium, I transitioned from a software engineering leader to a consultant. My servant leadership skills grew further during this period. I learned to lead without authority.

I grew many entrepreneurial leadership skills when I cofounded T3Ci, The Tag Tracking Company. I learned flexibility, resilience, and tenacity when we had to pivot our company to become Retail Solutions. Here again, I had the unparalleled opportunity of working with some of the world's leaders in consumer packaged goods (CPG), such as Procter & Gamble, Unilever, Kraft, and PepsiCo. When we founded this company, none of us were experts in the retail domain. However, we learned from the best in the industry. Our company became a leader in retail analytics for the CPG sector. I also led a large Chinese team. I learned additional lessons in working with remote teams from other cultures. (I had also headed a distributed team in India during my time at Consilium.)

When I retired at the end of 2016, a whole world of new opportunities opened up to me. I wrote a book on pioneering women engineers of India, started a part-time mentoring job in innovation and entrepreneurship, and earned credits for public speaking. My listening and coaching skills grew by leaps and bounds as I plunged into mentoring the students at my undergraduate alma mater. In the last couple of years, I have been spending half my time advising my mentees on various aspects of work—leadership, education, and career management.

Leadership has gone through a lot of changes in the last couple of decades. We have come to realize that outstanding leadership is not about being authoritarian and exercising control. It is not about the intelligence quotient (IQ) but the emotional intelligence.[3] To be an outstanding leader, you need several essential skills. You can learn them with consistent practice. The more you write and speak, the more you will master the basics of communication, but how you communicate is entirely up to your emotional intelligence. What kind of communicator are you? Do you understand your audience? Is your communication situational? Do you know when you should be a forceful, direct communicator or when to be a sympathetic listener?

A Lifelong Love of The Beatles

> *The music you love when you're a teenager is always going to be the most important to you.*
>
> **—Lin-Manuel Miranda on Fresh Air, WHYY, January 2017**

I was 17 years old when I first listened to The Beatles and fell in love with the music.

While studying engineering, I stayed in a women's hostel. The resident student advisor was the only one with a radio, and some of us begged her to use it on Saturday nights when the Listener's Choice program came on All India Radio, Madras. The Beatles' songs from the program sounded magical. A lifelong fan was born. When my family in Madurai bought a record player, I jumped with joy. I could buy my favorite records with my scholarship money and take them home during holidays to play and share with my sisters. When my husband, daughter, and I left for the United States, I packed the few records I had in between my sarees, and I still have them today in my stereo cabinet. Over the years, I had bought the box set of all their albums on vinyl and CDs, and their songs dominate my Spotify playlist. I never saw The Beatles in person. I don't regret it, though. There is something intimate about listening to them alone, without all the noise and hoopla associated with live performances. When I turned 60, I asked my family to celebrate it at the Cirque du Soleil's "Love" show based on The Beatles, in Las Vegas. It was a memorable experience.

Now in my seventies, I love their music as much as I loved it when I was a teenager. When my granddaughter was old enough, I introduced her to "Strawberry Fields Forever," so we could sing along in the car. Instead of annoying, her repeated requests to listen to it delighted me. Now her twin brothers have become huge fans as well. The love continues.

The Beatles were leaders of the music industry. In the early days, they encountered many rejections. The *Anthology*, released in 2000, describes their rejection by Decca Records. The Beatles' manager, Brian Epstein, did not give up when he was told guitar groups were on the way out. He persuaded George Martin at EMI's Parlophone label to sign them. They took risks throughout their careers by experimenting with distinct elements of music. They devoted an enormous amount of time to their craft. Their performances during their early days in Hamburg, which stretched over eight-hour periods, are legendary. They embraced their differences and their individual strengths and weaknesses and created music that transcends generations of music lovers. Their music is timeless, just as certain principles of leadership are.

About This Book

Leadership is about inspiring yourself and others to achieve common goals. You can bring the essence of leadership into your life every day and motivate yourself. You can inspire those around you to be better versions of themselves.

I had thought about writing a book on business leadership for a while based on my experiences as a leader and entrepreneur. While there is no shortage of leadership books, I wanted my book to reflect my source of inspiration uniquely, which is the music of The Beatles.

If you are a fan of The Beatles, I hope you will find my association of leadership ideas to their song titles in this book inspirational, playful, thoughtful, and valuable. If not, whether you are an aspiring leader, a seasoned leader, or a student of leadership, I hope this book will introduce you to them.

I have organized each of the chapters in the book around one central message on a leadership attribute captured by a Beatles' song title. The engineer in me wanted to give you some tools, so in each chapter, there are sections on how to become better at hitting the target of the message. There is a suggestion for practice. There are questions to ask yourself to help you think about the topic and additional resources at the end of each chapter.

Sixteen titles from The Beatles' enormous collection of songs inspired my chapters on leadership. Each of these titles has an associative meaning for me. When I think about one of these titles, I think about a leadership characteristic. For example, the title "Get Back" makes me think of getting back to being curious, like when I was a child, and I am reminded of the importance of curiosity to leadership when that song is played. The chapters cover these topics:

Attributes:

- Optimism (Getting Better)
- Humility (Within You Without You)
- Tenacity (The Long and Winding Road)
- Curiosity (Get Back)
- Vulnerability (Help!)
- Thinking for yourself (Think for Yourself)

Skills:

- Communication (I Want to Tell You)
- Negotiation (We Can Work It Out)
- Being available (Any Time at All)
- Empowering your team (I Me Mine)
- Leading with love and compassion (All You Need Is Love)

Mastery:

- Using intuition (I've Got a Feeling)
- Managing leadership tensions (Hello, Goodbye)

Care:

- Handling stress (Let It Be)
- Lifelong learning (The Inner Light)
- Balancing work and family (When I'm Sixty-Four)

This book is for aspiring leaders, students of leadership, and enterprise managers at different levels—first-time, middle, senior. You can use the chapters as references for the situations you may come across in your leadership journey. The resources will help you explore a topic further. You can read the chapters in any order of your choice.

Happy reading!

Notes

1. Praise, shanthamohan.com, accessed June 9, 2021, https://shanthamohan.com/testimonial/
2. Robert K. Greenleaf, *The Servant as Leader* (The Greenleaf Center for Servant Leadership, 1970).
3. Daniel Goleman, *Emotional Intelligence: Why It Can Matter More Than IQ* (Bantam, 2006).

LEADERSHIP ATTRIBUTES

1

Chapter 1

Getting Better

The song "Getting Better" makes me feel optimistic when I listen to it. Leaders encounter many road-blocks in achieving their goals, and optimism keeps them going despite the need to deal with them. It helps them view every obstacle as an opportunity. Some are born optimists. For others, there are strategies you can use to build it up. In this chapter, we will look at the benefits of optimism and methods to improve it.

About the Song

"Getting Better," released in 1967, features in the album *Sgt. Pepper's Lonely Hearts Club Band.* The song includes several instruments, including the Indian tambura played by George, piano by George Martin, and hand clapping by all The Beatles. Paul wrote most of it, with some added lyrics by John.

DOI: 10.4324/9781003267546-2

Knowing how optimistic Paul is, you can guess who wrote which lines. The title is upbeat, but John's lyrics in this song talk about his dark past. When I listen to this song, I hear only optimism. I don't register the negativity, and I guess it is because I am an eternal optimist!

Getting Better—Optimism

> *The optimist sees the rose and not its thorns. The pessimist stares at the thorns, oblivious to the rose.*
>
> **—Khalil Gibran**[1]

As a leader, you encounter situations that test your abilities every day. A trusted colleague leaves the organization. A key customer stopped using your services. Revenue numbers don't meet the expectations for the quarter. The board wants you to take an exit you don't want to. A recruiting site reports a bad rating on your company's leadership. All these unforeseen situations can bring your spirits down.

Founders' Optimism

When my cofounders and I started Retail Solutions in 2003, we were going to harness the power of all the data generated by radio-frequency identification (RFID) and build a successful company. We called the company T3Ci (The Tag Tracking Company Inc.). That year, Walmart, a major retailer, required its suppliers to place RFID tags with electronic product codes on their products. We developed software that would read and understand RFID data, and retailers and their Consumer Packaged Goods (CPG) suppliers used the analytical insights we produced to improve sales, promotions, and out-of-stock (OOS) metrics. The company received venture funding and expanded its operations. We processed the billionth RFID tag-read in 2007, and by the end of the year, we served over 30 customers, including four of the top five CPG manufacturers.

Then calamity struck. Walmart ended its mandate. We encountered a problem that seemed insurmountable. We might have closed our operations, and that would have been the end of our start-up. But we did not. We pivoted. We acted quickly and acquired the Retail Data Services business unit of

VeriSign and formed Retail Solutions Inc. Instead of analyzing RFID tags, we now focused on point-of-sale (POS) data from retailers. We formed partnerships with major retailers and became leaders in CPG retail analytics domain.[2]

If we had given up, hundreds of our employees would have found themselves without jobs. Our investors would have suffered losses. Instead, we moved forward to find a solution to our problem. We recognized the positive aspects of T3Ci—our reputation, our dedication to service, and our customers who loved us and wanted us to succeed—and used those to our advantage. Our optimism helped us move past the obstacle.

Optimistic Leaders

Bill and Melinda Gates Foundation publishes an annual letter. They addressed the 2017 letter[3] to the investor and philanthropist, Warren Buffett, who inspires them. In this letter, they thanked Warren for his gift to the foundation. They talked about the activities undertaken and the progress they have seen in making life better for everyone worldwide. In the last 25 years, extreme poverty in the world has been cut in half. Yet, in a survey, 99% underestimated the achievement. Bill cites this and says the world needs more optimism. Melinda adds that we all need to have more optimism, but we cannot expect that things will be taken care of automatically. We need the drive and commitment to make things better and the conviction to succeed. She says this is something they find in Warren. His success is not the reason he is optimistic. Instead, his optimism made him successful.

Walt Disney, the founder of Disney animation movies and the Disney empire, was an optimistic leader. Do you know the story of the birth of the most adored animation character Mickey Mouse he created? After a failed business meeting in New York in 1928, Disney sent a telegram to his brother Roy, telling him not to worry, before boarding the train back to California. He said everything was okay and would provide the details in person. He didn't tell Roy that he tried to promote his existing popular character, Oswald the Lucky Rabbit, but lost his contract. The indomitable Disney sketched furiously on his three-day train journey back, and a brand-new character Mickey Mouse was born. The rest is history. Optimistic leaders don't give up in the face of difficulties but persevere. They are not just hopeful but have the will to turn that hope into reality. The cliched sayings such as "if you get a lemon, make lemonade" or "instead of looking at the glass as half empty, see that it is half full" come to mind when describing their behavior. Such leaders are relentless in searching for new ideas and keeping an open mind about possibilities.

Optimism Benefits

A 2019 study[4] of 69,744 women and 1429 men found that of those who took part, those with more optimism are likely to live longer than 85 years. All the participants completed surveys on several factors, such as levels of optimism, overall health, diets, and habits, such as smoking and drinking. The women took part in the survey for 10 years, and the men for 30 years. The study validated the results by considering age, level of education, illnesses, etc. On average, optimistic people have 11–15% longer life than those with lower levels of optimism, the study found. We are not sure why optimism helps people live longer. Perhaps they don't give up and take care of themselves. They progress in their life journeys cheerfully, even when faced with setbacks.

Optimistic leaders are successful for many reasons. The stories of many outstanding leaders, such as Walt Disney, tell us they are problem-solvers. They work to overcome roadblocks. Failures don't get them down, and they deal with them much better than those who are pessimistic. They take complete responsibility for their decisions and are not afraid to take risks. Optimists are hopeful about what the future might bring. As Melinda said, they not only have hope but work to make it a reality. Leaders with positive attitudes make their entire team optimistic. Their actions and communication convey the can-do-spirit to their teams and inspire them.

Building Optimism

Some are born optimists. I am one of them. If you are not, let's look at some strategies to increase your optimism.

There are two theories of optimism. One of them, called dispositional theory (or trait theory), says it is a built-in characteristic. This trait drives everything that happens to the person, such as mental and physical well-being. The other one is the explanatory theory. Its foundation is based on how one mentally explains the events that happen to them. Martin Seligman[5] is a proponent of the explanatory style theory of optimism. He says pessimists can change their ways to become optimists, based on his previous work on "learned helplessness."[6]

It helps to understand the difference between pessimists and optimists in how they react to an adverse event. We can describe this on a spectrum of permanence, pervasiveness, and personalization (Figure 1.1).

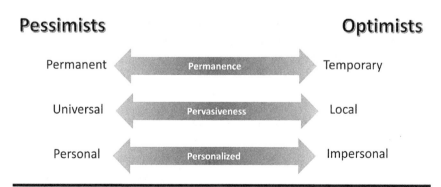

Figure 1.1   Optimist–pessimist continuum.

A pessimist treats a defeat as permanent, while an optimist thinks it is temporary. When encountered with setbacks, a pessimist perceives he is a total failure, but an optimist treats them as something specific to the setback. A pessimist personalizes setbacks by blaming herself. On the contrary, the optimist believes the environment is at fault.

Let's review an example of a setback that two leaders experience. One of them is optimistic, and the other is pessimistic.

Imagine the setback as losing a customer. Consider how each of the leaders would react to this setback. The optimistic leader would consider it as a misfortune. She would not blame herself. The loss of the customer would make her analyze the problem, and she would come up with a plan of action to get the customer back and safeguard against other such failures. But the pessimistic leader would blame herself and consider the setback as permanent. She would feel dejected and not attempt to win the customer back. The feeling of failure would permeate everything she does.

Even extreme optimists may not react with utmost positive reactions under some setbacks. Yet, because they are optimists, they can overcome any temporary negative responses.

The ABCDE Method

For an aspiring leader, the challenge is to move from left to right on the above spectrum and build optimism. You can do so with the use of the *ABCDE* method.[7] This was advocated initially by Ellis and Dryden and later refined by Seligman. The first element of this method identifies the setback or adverse event that starts our thinking or belief (*A*). How we feel about the setback, our belief (*B*), is the second element. How we respond to an event based on our view of the event is the consequence (*C*). Questioning the initial thought is the fourth element, the disputation (*D*). The last element is the outcome of trying to challenge our belief (*E*).

Let's walk through an example.

Backdrop: Andrea is a software engineering leader with several releases to her credit. Her company wants to expand its product portfolio. Andrea has been asked to provide a proposal to support the plan. She analyzes the scenario and realizes that to create the new products, her engineering team, which has a staff of 50, needs new skills and new talent. Andrea comes up with a proposal for expanding her global engineering team. When she submits the proposal, the CEO tells her that the other functional stakeholders don't support her plan.

Here is how the set of five elements of the ABCDE method unfold:

1. My colleagues in the C-team did not accept my plan for the engineering team's expansion. (Adversity)
2. I am not good at planning. My peers don't like me. (Belief)
3. Instead of trying to change the plan with the feedback, give up on expanding the team. (Consequence)
4. I have done this so many times. I must have overlooked some key aspects. What did I miss? (Disputation or question)
5. Let me talk to my colleagues to understand their objections better. Then, I can propose a new plan. Giving up is not an option. (Energization)

The fourth step, disputation, is the crucial step in breaking pessimism. You can use four ways to execute this step: find evidence (1), search for alternatives (2), identify implications (3), or ask if the belief is valid (4).

(1) Finding evidence is about gathering facts to examine your belief. In the above example, evidence would be that Andrea has many years of experience in building her

team from scratch. The team couldn't have grown to the current state without her being good at it, and Andrea's proposals were never rejected outright. When you gather evidence, you may realize that your belief doesn't quite stand up.

(2) Alternatives help you view the setback and question your initial belief. Can you view the setback differently? In the above example, instead of personalizing it, Andrea might explore why her proposal was rejected. Perhaps she wasn't eloquent in stating her reasons for expansion. Or she missed providing convincing background material that supports expanding engineering.

(3) Implications examine if the belief is true. What if Andrea is not good at planning? Can she rectify it? What if her colleagues don't like her? Can she do something about it? Implications help Andrea find ways to learn and grow.

(4) Usefulness is about examining the belief to explore if it is helpful to you. In the example, if Andrea believes this is not useful, she can cast aside the thought and create an action plan to address the setback.

Often, we may use a mix of all these four ways to overcome the pessimist in us.

Avoiding Pessimism

Even the most optimistic leader could encounter situations that trigger pessimistic thoughts. How do you avoid these? By setting aside things which you cannot change. Have you heard about the serenity prayer?[8] "God, grant me the serenity to accept the things I cannot change, courage to change the things I can, and wisdom to know the difference." The last line in this prayer is critical. It would be too easy to throw up your hands and say you cannot change a situation, but you need to analyze it carefully to understand what is possible.

Avoid focusing on the setback and move forward with what you can do.

Back to the story about my start-up—we didn't dwell on the situation that Walmart abandoned its mandate about implementing RFID; instead, we moved forward with a plan to keep the venture alive.

To grow your optimism, practice the ABCDE method by keeping track of your adverse events as they occur and be diligent about applying the disputation step. Besides practicing the ABCDE method, realize that your environment has a lot of impact on your behavior. If pessimists surround you, try to spend as little time as possible with them. Find people who have a positive attitude and cultivate those relationships.

Optimism and Realism

"Peanuts" is a celebrated comic strip by Charles M. Schulz.[9] In it, the main character Charlie Brown and his friend Lucy have a recurring theme. When Charlie comes running to kick the football Lucy is holding, she takes it away, and Charlie falls on his back. Charlie is undaunted by his defeat. Ever the optimist, he continues to hope that he will kick the ball in the next attempt.

In my start-up, we experienced something akin to this story. We sold our services to enterprises. The sales involved many stakeholders—the budget holder, the implementor, and the end user. One of our top customers would ask us to execute special research and development projects repeatedly. Every time he asked, we spent substantial effort in preparing the proposals. But time and time again, the customer would postpone signing the contract with some excuse. We were tired of his habit of raising our hopes, only to see it dashed when pressed for a contract. One of our cofounders found humor in this situation. After several such attempts at securing a contract, he sent us an email with the subject, "Lucy strikes again." We learned a valuable lesson. We asked to speak to the budget-holder first in special project contracts.

Interestingly, I read that there have been many variations of this strip, named "Football Gag." The strip published on October 16, 1983, showed Charlie walking away when Lucy dares him to kick the ball, only to see many others waiting for him to kick the balls they are holding!

Leaders need to temper optimism with reality. Optimism needs to be accompanied by other attributes of leadership, including results. In his article "The Leadership Advantage,"[10] Warren Bennis lays out the characteristics of exemplary leadership as serving the needs of the followers. A leader must foster hope and optimism that will sustain her team, besides providing a purpose. She must inspire trust and expect results (Figure 1.2).

As a leader, learn to use your enthusiasm to meet the expectations of your team and give them the confidence to move forward. Your team needs to realize that you are competent, caring, and authentic. Optimism is necessary, but it is not sufficient. A sense of purpose and results-oriented mentality must accompany the confidence that things will work out.

Exemplary Leadership

To satisfy followers' needs and achieve positive outcomes leaders must address four needs

In Service of Constituent needs for:	Leaders Provide:	To Help Create:
Meaning and Direction	Sense of Purpose	Goals and objectives
Trust	Authentic relationships	Reliability and consistency
Hope and Optimism	"Hardiness" (confidence that things will workout)	Energy and commitment
Results	Bias toward action, risk, curiosity, and courage	Confidence and creativity

Figure 1.2   Exemplary leadership. (Adapted from Leadership Advantage.)

It Is Getting Better

Optimism is contagious. When a leader tells her team, "You can do it," the team members are inspired and energized to overcome hurdles and do their best to achieve results. Balancing that optimism with realism and being prepared for whatever may come is the best strategy you can use to become an influential leader.

To Practice

- Next time when someone proposes a new idea, note your immediate reaction to it. Stop being dismissive by saying, "That won't work." Instead, find ways in which the proposal can succeed.
- When you encounter a setback, apply the ABCDE method. Do this for the subsequent four or five setbacks. Keep a record of what you did in your disputation step in each of these setbacks. Reflect on it and find insights that can help you with your next one.

Optimism—Questions to Ask Yourself

- Do I question my negative beliefs?
- Do I celebrate minor victories?
- Do I understand my strengths and leverage them?

Notes

1. Khalil Gibran, *The Kahlil Gibran Reader: Inspirational Writings* (Copyright: Philosophical Library, Kensington Publishing Corporation, 2006).
2. Retail Solutions Inc., Wikipedia, accessed June 8, 2021, https://en.wikipedia.org/wiki/Retail_Solutions_Inc.
3. "Our 2017 Annual Letter," GatesNotes, 2017, accessed June 8, 2021, https://www.gatesnotes.com/2017-Annual-Letter.

4. Boston University School of Medicine, "New Evidence that Optimists Live Longer: After Decades of Research, a New Study Links Optimism and Prolonged Life," *ScienceDaily*, accessed June 8, 2021, www.sciencedaily.com/releases/2019/08/190826150700.htm.
5. Martin E.P. Seligman, *Learned Optimism: How to Change Your Mind and Your Life* (Pocket Books, 1991).
6. Christopher Peterson, et al., *Learned Helplessness: A Theory for the Age of Personal Control* (Freeman, 1975).
7. Albert Ellis & Windy Dryden, *The Practice of Rational-Emotive Therapy (RET)* (Springer Publishing Co., 1987).
8. "Serenity Prayer," Wikipedia, accessed October 20, 2021, https://en.wikipedia.org/wiki/Serenity_Prayer.
9. "Peanuts," Wikipedia, accessed September 2, 2021, https://en.wikipedia.org/wiki/Peanuts.
10. Warren Bennis, "Leadership Advantage," *Leader to Leader*, University of Pittsburgh Executive Forum, Vol. 1999, No. 12 (Spring 1999): 18–23, Wiley Online Library, November 8, 2006, accessed September 2021, https://onlinelibrary.wiley.com/doi/10.1002/ltl.40619991205.

Resources

Alan Loy McGinnis, *The Power of Optimism* (HarperCollins, 1990).
Martin E.P. Seligman, *Learned Optimism: How to Change Your Mind and Your Life* (Free Press, 2006).

Chapter 2

Within You Without You

Humble leaders take their organizations to great heights. Studies show that humility fosters collaboration, knowledge sharing, and collective achievement in a team. You can become such a leader by using introspection (go "within you") and letting go of your ego (go "without you"). As a modest leader, you don't care about taking credit for an accomplishment. When you communicate, it is about "we" and "us," and not "I" and "me." You are not afraid of saying, "I don't know." For you, the team comes first. Humility stands on the pillars of self-awareness, gratitude, integrity, learning, and listening. You can develop it by consciously exercising all these attributes.

About the Song

Recorded and released in 1967, "Within You Without You" appeared on *Sgt. Pepper's Lonely Hearts Club*

DOI: 10.4324/9781003267546-3

Band. George Harrison composed the song on a harmonium and this was the only song by him to appear on that album. I am a huge fan of George, perhaps because of his affinity for Indian music and instruments. This song resonates with me in a big way, and the leaders I admire are those who are humble while leading their immensely successful teams.

Within You Without You—Humility

Humble leaders have the hearts and minds of their followers.

The song "Within You Without You" is supposedly about the metaphysical space that divides us. But when I listen to this song, I hear the words that say we are all small compared to the universe, and life goes on without us—the ultimate humility.

What Kind of Leader Do You Want to Be?

I have come across many leaders who exhibit so much self-importance that holding a conversation with them is painful. Everything is about their accomplishments, all about their thoughts, and you cannot get a word edgewise. I also know of leaders who are as accomplished and as successful but are genuinely interested in listening to others and don't think that the sun rises and sets only for them. Which leader would you rather follow? Which leader would you rather be?

Outstanding leaders understand that our time in this world is limited. They want to live purposefully. They strive every day to make themselves better and make the lives of everyone around them better. Egotistical leaders consider themselves above everyone else. They believe they comprehend everything and stop learning and growing. These leaders create a barrier between themselves and others by their behavior and expect to win at all costs. They possess a false sense of security and put their organizations at risk by their unwillingness to listen to sound judgment.

A study of 105 small-to-medium-sized firms in the computer software and hardware industry in the United States[1] supported the hypothesis: when a humble CEO leads a firm, the executive management team is more likely to be collaborators, sharing information, empowering their teams, and driving to a shared vision resulting in better performance. In the paper, the authors say there are three themes involved in defining humility in business leadership. The first is self-awareness; the second is an open mind and a growth mindset; and the third is the appreciation for others' contributions.

Story of Jungkiu Choi

In his article, "How Humble Leadership Really Works,"[2] Dan Cable, author of *Alive at Work*, recounts the story of Jungkiu Choi, who moved from Singapore to China to lead Consumer Banking at Standard Chartered. His immediate responsibility was to persuade the branch managers to cut costs. When he started visiting the branches, he did so without announcing it. Instead of making the meetings formal and authoritative, he made them casual. He served breakfast to the employees, met with them, and solicited input on minimizing costs. While skeptical at first, the employees became comfortable and offered several suggestions that could help. Cable says that one such huddle yielded the innovative idea of synchronizing the branch hours with the hours of the mall where it was situated instead of having its own hours, producing weekend income that exceeded the weekly income of the branch in a few months.

Characteristics of Humble Leaders

Several characteristics define a leader with humility (Figure 2.1).

They are self-aware and derive their strength from within themselves. When humble leaders receive praise, it thrills them, but even without it, within their hearts, they recognize it when they do something useful. They don't care how many "likes" they get on a social media platform. They go about leading quietly.

Figure 2.1   Characteristics of a humble leader.

Leaders with humility don't compare themselves to others. They also see that while they can do anything, they cannot do everything all at once. They know that being authentic is critical to achieving any goal.

Humble leaders do not care about taking credit, but they willingly share the credit with those who work with them. They take ownership of failures. Jim Collins, the author of the book *Good to Great*,[3] explains this characteristic as looking away from ourselves, looking out the window to give credit, and looking at ourselves, looking in the mirror to take the blame. The humble leader not only accepts their own mistakes but also owns the mistakes of the entire organization.

Own Your Mistakes

During the pandemic, the video conferencing tool Zoom became the default platform for connecting with the office and friends and working from home. As the usage of Zoom increased, security and privacy issues surfaced. Eric Yuan, the CEO of Zoom, released a statement,[4] apologized for the lack of controls, and spoke to the media. He said how privileged his company was to help everyone stay connected during the pandemic and the immense responsibility that accompanied it. More to the point, he said, they met neither their own expectations nor that of the community regarding security and privacy. He talked about the efforts underway to prevent the issues. Yuan acknowledged they moved too quickly and followed up his message with actions to rectify the shortcomings. The statement accepted the problem faced by the company, and the apology took responsibility for the situation.

Share Acclaim

Art Gensler, his wife Drue, and James Follett cofounded the world's largest architecture firm, Gensler,[5] in 1965. It had a humble beginning in interior design. The firm grew to design universities, hotels, and sports stadia. It designed corporate headquarters of companies such as Facebook, Hyundai, several US domestic airports, and international airports. Gensler designed China's tallest skyscraper— Shanghai Tower, one of the notable buildings. Art attributed his success to his clients. He said they not only gave the firm opportunities to grow. They also acted as cheerleaders, encouraging growth nationally and worldwide. A CNN article[6] said he never wanted his buildings to be celebrated as "Art Gensler buildings."

Sharing acclaim is a hallmark of a humble leader. Teams under a leader with humility thrive because the leader gives them all the support needed to become better and achieve more. They trust the leader who inspires them to work in harmony. When teams succeed, the leaders experience tremendous joy.

Listen

Humble leaders are proficient in listening. They don't like the sound of their own voices. They reflect on what they learned and take action. Indra Nooyi, the CEO of PepsiCo between 2006 and 2018, described the leadership lessons she learned at PepsiCo in a LinkedIn article.[7] She talked about the need for a vision, long-term focus, the importance of persuasion, the importance of listening, and being a lifelong learner. On listening, she recounted the story of learning ballroom dancing and the instructor's advice. The instructor told her he struggled to teach her because Indra was trying to lead instead of following. He advised her to learn to follow. You become a better leader by listening and learning to follow, and you become a better dancer, too—a profound lesson! Indra says we need to listen more to the surrounding wisdom.

Learn

Leaders with healthy ego don't claim to know it all but are aware of their accomplishments. Their communication conveys confidence along with humility. In 2014, Rajiv Suri became the CEO of Nokia. In his letter to the employees,[8] he spoke about how excited and honored he was to take on this responsibility. He had learned something new at every role he had previously held at Nokia, he said. Suri expressed his desire to leverage opportunities that the new role brought him and create value. The employees of Nokia heard him say that he seeks their help in fulfilling his responsibilities. Here is a leader who was sure of himself and his ability to lead, yet humble enough to say he had a lot to learn. His communication made everyone in his organization feel valuable. If team members get such an inspirational message, you can bet they will give their 100% support to the leader.

The Will to Succeed

In the chapter on optimism, I talk about combining it with realism to become an outstanding leader. In the same way, you need to blend humility with a strong will to succeed to become an exceptional leader.

Jim Collins, a researcher, author, speaker, and management consultant, coined the term "Level 5 Leadership" in his book *Good to Great*. He and his team conducted a study in which they looked at 1435 companies. They wanted to understand how companies with below-average results become excellent after business transformation. The study concluded that great companies prioritized sustaining growth over the long term. They committed themselves to excellence at every step of the way. The CEOs of these companies did not seek the limelight.[9] They were humble and put the good of the organization above their individual needs. But they also had an enormous drive to succeed.

Achieving a "Level 5 Leadership" requires mastery of the other four levels. These include the ability to lead your team with insights, skills, strong work ethic, performance orientation, and high standards in moving toward the clearly articulated vision. Get these under your belt and focus on achieving success with humility.

Learning Humility

Can you learn humility? Of course, you can. You can master it by building on the pillars of self-awareness, gratitude, integrity, learning, and listening (Figure 2.2).

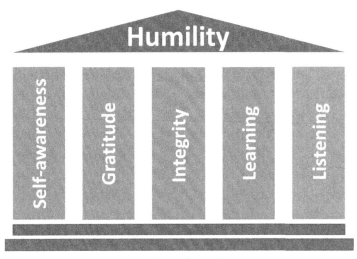

The Pillars of Humility

Figure 2.2 Pillars of humility.

Self-Awareness

If you Google "How do you develop self-awareness," you will find over a billion search results. The question is that popular. Self-awareness is the first of four main realms that make up our emotional intelligence (EI), which is defined as the ability to understand our own emotions and those of others in order to influence them. A leader who possesses a high degree of EI can lead her team to achieve superior results. The other three realms are self-management, social awareness, and relationship management. To cultivate EI, you must first be self-aware, and it is also the first pillar over which you can build humility. Self-awareness is looking at yourself honestly and seeing who you are—your strengths, weaknesses, values, passions, aspirations, and emotions.

In understanding your emotions, you take the first step by labeling them, says Susan David, the Harvard/McLean Institute of Coaching founder. In her article,[10] she provides many tips on how to use multiple labels, dig deeper into each to understand the nuances, and advocates writing them down and reflecting on them. Once you know your emotions, you will know underlying reasons and get clarity on your behavior. Do you act arrogantly? Do you have an exaggerated sense of yourself? At the other extreme, do you lack self-esteem? Do you always put yourself down?

New York Times bestselling author and organizational psychologist Tasha Eurich[11] says it is not enough to gain internal self-awareness. You should also have external self-awareness—how others perceive you. That is possible only when you are open to feedback and see yourself through the eyes of others. Once you are self-aware, you gain confidence in your abilities and accept your weaknesses to improve your humility.

Gratitude

A great way to become humble is by learning to be grateful. In a study to establish the relationship between expressing gratitude and humility,[12] the researchers proposed three hypotheses that, taken together, show humility and gratitude coexist in a virtuous cycle. They tested the hypotheses in two experiments and a 14-day diary study and concluded that a strong link between humility and gratitude exists. When the individuals were grateful, this fostered humble thoughts. Humility triggered grateful behaviors. We need additional research to understand this critical component of personal development.

Gratitude helps you develop positive relationships. If you are grateful to others for your accomplishments, you accept that you need their support. This acknowledgment builds humility. Don't take your team for granted. Show gratitude for everything they bring. It helps you and your team become more successful at everything you do.

Gratitude is the key to all virtues.

Practicing gratitude can begin small. An email thanking a team member for a job well done, praise for another leader for collaborating on a project, appreciation of your spouse for supporting your efforts at work, rewarding a customer for being loyal—all these can help you build humility. Robert Emmons, a professor of psychology at the University of California, Davis, is a leading proponent of gratitude. He is also the founding editor-in-chief of *The Journal of Positive Psychology*. In his article, "Why Gratitude Is Good,"[13] Emmons calls out the many benefits of gratitude, namely physical, mental, and social, the last one being very important for developing good relationships. He advocates keeping a gratitude journal as the number one way to practice gratitude. Emmons says, remembering the bad times, and comparing where you are now, can trigger feelings of gratitude.

Integrity

A leader with integrity doesn't worry about anyone looking over her shoulder. She doesn't care if someone will praise or condemn her and does the right thing because of her courage of conviction. She doesn't compromise her standards and values even in the face of disasters and builds credibility and trust with her collaborators. For a business leader, these are your employees, customers, partners, and investors. You develop a reputation as someone accountable. Since the leader with integrity always strives to do the right thing, humility becomes a natural part of the behavior.

An honest leader tries very hard to keep the commitments she makes. When she doesn't live up to them, she is open about it and shares it with the team. She praises those who are courageous and own their mistakes.

Learning

When you are leading a team or an organization, you are doing so because you are well-informed and perceptible. But in this ever-changing world, there is always more to understand. Humility begins with accepting how little we know. Humble leaders recognize that their schooling never stops. They are lifelong learners, willing to accept that they may not have all the answers. They are open to receiving insights from others, just as Jungkiu Choi did when he took the leadership of Consumer Banking at Standard Chartered. When you are sincerely ready to learn, you become humble. Many avenues open up to you for enhancing your knowledge, such as your professional network or mentor. Share your knowledge, and by modeling behaviors that promote collaboration, you inspire your team members to do the same.

Listening

Listening is fundamental to building humility. When we listen to others, we are giving importance to the person who is talking. A humble leader seeks opportunities for listening. When you walk around the workplace talking to your team members and peers, you create the means to exercise your skills. Spend more time outside your office. Engage in casual conversations. Share any new information you learned about the organization. Ask them about their work and find out what obstacles stand in the way of accomplishing their tasks. Discuss ways in which they can circumvent them. Listening doesn't stop with hearing, and you need to follow up with action. When you worry about responding to the person talking, it isn't easy to understand what is being said. Give yourself time to absorb what you heard. Active listening requires practice. If you keep at it, you will get better.

Be a Humble Leader with Ambition

You achieve outstanding results when you are humble and have a strong will to succeed. Put your team first and support them in achieving organizational excellence. You can build humility on the pillars of self-awareness, gratitude, integrity, learning, and listening. Teach yourself all these characteristics. Continually exercise them, and strive to be an ambitious leader with personal humility.

Practice

- Keep a gratitude journal.
- Write or email personal notes to your team members, thanking them for supporting you in achieving the organization's goals.
- Talk to your team in informal settings. If you work with remote teams, use tools such as phone, Slack, Zoom, Teams, or WebEx to reach out.

Humility—Questions to Ask Yourself

- Do I think consciously about my strengths and weaknesses?
- When was the last time I learned from my mistake?
- Do I empathize with those at work?
- What three things am I grateful for today?

Notes

1. Amy Y. Ou, et al., "Do Humble CEOs Matter? An Examination of CEO Humility and Firm Outcomes," *Journal of Management* (2015), https://doi.org/10.1177/0149206315604187.
2. Dan Cable, "How Humble Leadership Really Works," *Harvard Business Review*, April 23, 2018, accessed June 11, 2021, https://hbr.org/2018/04/how-humble-leadership-really-works.

3. Jim Collins, "Good to Great: Why Some Companies Make the Leap and Others Don't," *Harper Business*, October 16, 2001. Copyright © 2001 by Jim Collins, Reprinted by permission of Curtis Brown, Ltd.

4. Eric S. Yuan, "A Message to Our Users," *Zoom Blog*, April 1, 2020, accessed June 11, 2021, https://blog.zoom.us/a-message-to-our-users/.

5. Gensler, accessed July 20, 2021, https://www.gensler.com/.

6. CNN: Architecture, "Art Gensler, Founder of the World's Largest Architecture Firm, Has Died Aged 85," *CNN Style*, May 12, 2021, accessed July 20, 2021, https://www.cnn.com/style/amp/art-gensler-death/index.html.

7. Indra Nooyi, "'Leave the Crown in the Garage': What I've Learned from a Decade of Being PepsiCo's CEO," *LinkedIn*, July 31, 2017, accessed August 19, 2021, https://www.linkedin.com/pulse/leave-crown-garage-what-ive-learned-from-decade-being-indra-nooyi/.

8. Gyana Ranjan Swain, "Nokia CEO Rajeev Suri's Inspirational Letter to Its Employees," *TeleAnalysis*, April 30, 2014, accessed June 11, 2021, https://www.teleanalysis.com/nokia-ceo-rajeev-suris-letter-to-employees/.

9. Jim Collins, "Level 5 Leadership," accessed July 8, 2021, https://www.jimcollins.com/concepts/level-five-leadership.html.

10. Susan David, "3 Ways to Better Understand Your Emotions," *Harvard Business Review*, November 10, 2016, accessed June 20, 2021, https://hbr.org/2016/11/3-ways-to-better-understand-your-emotions.

11. Tasha Eurich, "What Self-Awareness Really Is (and How to Cultivate It)," *Harvard Business Review*, January 4, 2018, accessed June 9, 2021, https://hbr.org/2018/01/what-self-awareness-really-is-and-how-to-cultivate-it.

12. Elliott Kruse, et al., "An Upward Spiral between Gratitude and Humility," *Social Psychological and Personality Science*, Vol. 5, No. 7 (2014): 805. https://doi.org/10.1177/1948550614534700.

13. Robert Emmons, "Why Gratitude Is Good," *Greater Good Magazine*, November 16, 2010, accessed October 4, 2021, https://greatergood.berkeley.edu/article/item/why_gratitude_is_good.

Resources

Jim Collins, *Good to Great: Why Some Companies Make the Leap and Others Don't* (Harper Business, 2001).

Peter A. Schein & Edgar Schein, *Humble Leadership: The Power of Relationships, Openness, and Trust* (Berrett-Koehler Publishers, 2018).

Chapter 3

The Long and Winding Road

The journey of a leader is a long and winding road. It has many twists and turns. A leader must be able to navigate them. Tenacity, a critical leadership skill, can be helpful. Learn to be flexible and resilient. Characteristics such as grit, passion, and audacity will help you become a tenacious leader, and you can develop each of them with time and practice.

About the Song

"The Long and Winding Road" was released as a single in the United States in May 1970. It was The Beatles' last number one hit on the Billboard Hot 100 chart there. Paul McCartney, the author of this song, apparently wrote it in 1968 when staying in Scotland, imagining it would be a perfect song for Ray Charles. It features in the *Let It Be* album.

DOI: 10.4324/9781003267546-4

The Long and Winding Road—Tenacity

A tenacious leader trains for a marathon.

Everyone sees Elon Musk as the successful founder of Tesla and SpaceX. But do you know how many failures he overcame before he became successful? In the 1990s, he failed to get a job at Netscape, a Silicon Valley company. In 1996, he had to leave Zip2, a company he started. The investor and cofounder of the company PayPal fired him as CEO in 2000. In 2006, his first rocket launch exploded. In 2008, his companies Tesla and SpaceX were about to collapse. Both ventures have seen many setbacks. Tesla experienced several production failures, and SpaceX has seen many explosions. You can read about his spectacular failures in the press, including an infographic.[1] But his company Tesla reached a market cap of $572.99 billion on December 10, 2020. That success did not happen overnight. It proved to be a long road, with lessons from every failure.

A Tenacious Trailblazer

Michelle Payne grew up on a farm in Australia, the youngest of 10 children. As a child, she aspired to be a winning jockey, and her dream since the age of seven was to win the Melbourne Cup. She started racing when 15, following the footsteps of her older siblings. Michelle realized her dream by winning the Melbourne Cup in 2015. She became the first woman to win the race in its 155-year history.

Michelle's road to this victory teaches us about persistence. Throughout her racing years, she endured horrible falls. One of these fractured her skull and left her with bleeding on the brain. Her family tried to persuade her to give up racing without success. Another fall in 2012 resulted in four fractured vertebrae and broken ribs. Later that year, she experienced another nasty fall. Michelle didn't let these falls deter her from achieving her goal of winning the Melbourne Cup. She got back on the saddle as soon as she could and trained hard to get to where she wanted to go. Today, Michelle is a trainer, helping others in the field she loves.

The Starbucks Story

Howard Schultz, born to immigrant parents in 1953, grew up in Brooklyn, New York, in a public housing project. His parents were not college-educated. His father worked as a laborer to support the family, and they were not too well-off. Schultz found escape in sports. He played football in his high school and hoped to get a sports scholarship for college. Though he didn't get a scholarship, he started attending Northern Michigan University with the support of student loans and part-time jobs. Schultz joined an office equipment company after graduating in 1975 and became good at selling door-to-door. He then joined a European houseware company after working for a few more companies. In 1982, he visited his customer, Starbucks, a small coffee company in Seattle. That visit turned into a job at Starbucks as head of marketing.

On a business trip to Italy in 1983, Schultz became enamored with the espresso beverage and the cafe ambiance. When he returned to Seattle, he encouraged the owners of Starbucks to adopt his ideas of serving espresso and making Starbucks into cafes. The owners didn't support the idea. Schultz left the company to pursue his dream, even though he had no funds. Investors shot down his request for funding over 200 times. Can you imagine being turned down so many times? His early years of selling sure helped him be persistent. Finally, he raised funds and opened "Il Giornale," his dream store. Two years later, the owners of Starbucks decided to focus on another part of the business, and Schultz bought Starbucks and merged with Il Giornale to create the new company. He spent over 40 years growing Starbucks from a few stores to over 20,000 stores globally. Schultz never forgot the obstacles he overcame, including his humble beginnings. Under his leadership, Starbucks became a company that gave stock ownership to all employees. In 2018, he became chair emeritus of Starbucks.

The Pandemic Hero

Dr. Katalin Kariko's story epitomizes tenacity. She is a hero of the pandemic war for laying the groundwork for the COVID-19 vaccine development with her work on Messenger RNA (mRNA).[2] Born in Hungary in 1955, Kariko dreamed of being a scientist. She received her Ph.D. in Hungary and worked in many labs, both there and in the United States. A *New York Times* article[3] said her career at the University of Pennsylvania was tenuous. Her earnings were modest, and she relied on senior scientists in different labs to support her work.

Kariko spent many years trying to use the power of mRNA to combat diseases. This idea was not popular in the 1990s.[4] Her colleagues didn't support it, and no corporation or government funded the research. But Kariko never gave up believing that her work on mRNA would help medicine. This belief included vaccine production, and it bore fruit several years later. We owe the COVID-19 vaccine to Kariko and a few others.

Dr. David Langer, MD, chair of neurosurgery at Lenox Hill Hospital, said this on Twitter[5]:

> @katekariko is a superstar. She went through such hardship and overcame so much. I saw it and witnessed her supreme work ethic and focus and always doing what was right against all odds. She deserves a tremendous amount of gratitude from us all.

Keep an Open Mind

There are times you need to accept that no matter how much you persist, the outcome is not what you want. In his book,

Loonshots: How to Nurture the Crazy Ideas That Win Wars, Cure Diseases, and Transform Industries,[6] Safi Bahcall defines a phrase, "Listen to the Suck with Curiosity (LSC)." It is about overcoming the urge to quit when confronted with the failure of an idea. Instead, you keep an open mind and investigate the failure. Safi says LSC is a signal for how one tells the difference between stubbornness and persistence.

Your understanding of what caused the failure is the first step in continuing to work on your idea. Perhaps, instead of quitting, you need to reframe the problem and be flexible. In entrepreneurship, changing your goals, or pivoting, is common. Retail Solutions, the company I cofounded, initially focused on RFID (radio-frequency identification) data and analytics. The venture floundered since the technology was not appropriate for the retail domain at the time. Instead of persisting with that idea, we pivoted. We began to address the market with readily available data.

The case of Shopify is another entrepreneurship example in which tenacity paid off. In 2004, it was a failing online snowboard equipment company. The founders had spent a lot of effort in building their e-commerce site to sell their equipment. They decided to stop selling the equipment. Instead, they pivoted and turned their e-commerce site into a platform as a service to other vendors. Shopify is now a leading e-commerce platform, with over 800,000 online stores.

Think Out of the Box

A great lesson on learning to be tenacious by being nimble comes from the story of Wrigley's gum. In 1891, William Wrigley Jr. sold soap in Chicago.[7] He found that the profit margins of soap were low. He offered some freebies. One of these freebies was baking powder. This combination of soap and baking powder seemed to sell very well since baking

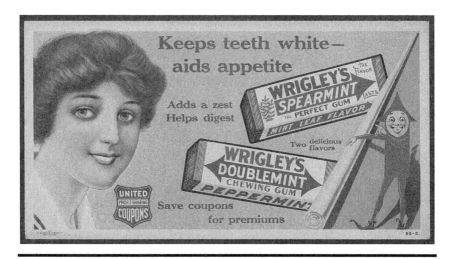

Figure 3.1   Ad card from 1915 with health benefits. (Image courtesy of Wrigley Archives.)

happened to be a popular activity around the time. Then he started selling baking powder as a stand-alone product. William offered two packs of gum with each packet of baking powder to help increase sales. Before he knew it, chewing gum became very popular. The financial crisis of 1907 brought a pivot to Wrigley's gum—this time in marketing. William recognized that gum is an impulse buy. It needed to become a habit so that chewing gum could become a regular buy. He decided to market the product promoting its health benefits. The advertisements in the 1910s started emphasizing the health benefits, such as clean teeth and digestive aid (Figure 3.1).

Building Tenacity

How do you learn to be tenacious? How do you learn to pivot? The first step is to become self-aware. Instead of focusing on the environment, look at yourself. Compare yourself with your standards of what you would like to be. Then specify for yourself how you ought to think, feel, and behave, and you will

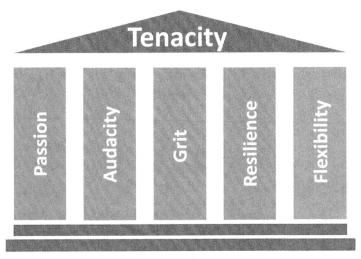

The Pillars of Tenacity

Figure 3.2   Pillars of tenacity.

start to self-correct your behavior. Let's say you didn't get the outcome you wanted in a negotiation. If you are self-aware, you would ask yourself what you could have done differently. You would take responsibility for it. You would remember to negotiate better next time.

You build tenacity over time by exercising your passion, audacity, grit, resilience, and flexibility (Figure 3.2).

Passion

Passion is fundamental to building tenacity. You will never achieve your aspirations if you don't care about what you do. For most of us, passion is something we cannot comprehend without some exploration. Passion is looking forward to something constantly. It is not something you can develop by reading or dreaming. Passion requires action.

When you are leading, passion is something that matters to you and your team. A passionate leader inspires her followers and creates support for her vision. An intense desire drives the leaders and their teams to have courage and the grit to keep going in the face of failures. Kariko's story we saw earlier exemplifies this. The singular focus for mRNA research in curing diseases carried her through many years of hard work, leading to the invention of a vaccine for COVID-19.

Audacity

I am not afraid of storms, for I am learning how to sail my ship.

—*Little Women*, Louisa May Alcott

Audacity is another word for taking risks. If you never take risks, you will never understand the meaning of failure. You will never develop tenacity. Leaders must have the courage to stand up for their principles, ideas, plans, and teams. You have heard the advice to do something every day that scares you. You can build courage day by day by following this advice. If you take minor risks every day, soon you will build up the courage to take bigger ones. For example, share your ideas in a meeting with your peers. Propose changes to an existing company policy. Ask someone you admire to be your mentor.

When you listen to stories of bravery, they inspire you. During the COVID-19 pandemic, we heard many inspirational stories from all over the world about courageous individuals who worked against incredible odds to help their fellow human beings. They had a multiplying effect by spurring on all of us to do what needed to be done.

Remember how Elon Musk is attempting to do what nobody has done before with his space explorations when you are afraid to take risks.

Grit

Angela Lee Duckworth is a psychologist, science author, professor and founder, and CEO of Character Lab. Her TED talk on grit, watched over 23 million times,[8] talks about her research on the characteristics that make someone success-ful. She and her team researched the candidates at West Point Military Academy. They wanted to understand which candi-date would stay in military training and who would drop out. In another study, they tried to predict which children would advance in the National Spelling Bee competition. The team also studied the characteristics of novice teachers in tough neighborhoods to see who would make the most impact on children. They worked with companies to understand which salespeople would be the most successful. The research find-ings pointed to grit, which Merriam Webster defines[9] as the firmness of mind or spirit—unyielding courage in the face of hardship or danger—the ability to pursue a goal relentlessly over a long period. Angela says the growth mindset advocated by Carol Dweck[10] can help develop grit. When you believe failure is something you can overcome, you keep going. You persevere.

You can learn grit with practice, time, and purpose. Milo of Croton was an ancient wrestler from Greece who was extraor-dinarily strong. He won multiple games in the Olympics at the time. His legendary strength seems to have come from his training, carrying a progressively heavier calf daily from its birth to its full size as an ox. Just like what it takes to develop muscle strength, you can grow grit with time and training.

Resilience

Resilience builds tenacity. Countless talks and articles discuss bouncing back from catastrophic events. But what can you do to help be resilient every day from the disappointments and setbacks? Researchers at University of Wisconsin conducted a study at Promega,[11] a biotechnology company, which pro-vided some answers. The study found that practicing mind-fulness improves your resiliency, and thus, your tenacity. The experimental group in the study received weekly training and practiced meditation at home for one hour a day for six days, while the control group did not receive any mindfulness training. A survey collected input from the participants on how they felt at the end of the eight-week study. In addition, measuring the electrical activity of the participants' brains showed increased levels of activity associated with calmness and positivity. We need to conduct more research to validate the findings of this study. But it is generally accepted that mindfulness has proven benefits. Practicing mindfulness can improve your resiliency, and thus, your tenacity.

Another way to improve resiliency is to conceptualize the traumatic events or setbacks we encounter as an opportunity to learn and grow.[12] Events become traumatic by how you construe them. By learning to construe them positively, you can become resilient. You can learn to better regulate your feelings by viewing them through the lens of opportunity to learn. Putting a positive spin on traumatic events can also help.

Flexibility

Flexibility is the characteristic of adapting readily to new situations. It is part of a growth mindset. The lack of flexibility denotes a fixed mindset. Flexibility takes you from being just stubborn to being persistent and gives you room to pivot if necessary. It allows you to explore the possibilities to overcome difficulties. Remind yourself about the story of Shopify mentioned earlier.

You can develop flexibility by asking yourself if you have a clear picture of your purpose and goal. Consider all the options that may be available to you. When you are stubborn, it might cause you to get stuck in a situation. Ask yourself what else you can do. Your regular activities can help you become flexible. Doing something different from how you have always done it in a certain way will build flexibility. For example, if you use a particular route in your walks, choose a different route. If you eat cereal every day, consider eating toast. Pursue new challenges and experiences. Meet new people.

Build Your Tenacity

The leadership journey is long and winding. It has many twists and turns that are unpredictable. Build your tenacity to make this journey successful. In this chapter, I talked about the pillars which help you do that. Each of these pillars requires practice. They are also symbiotic. Find your passion by exploring different options. Support that passion with grit, flexibility, audacity, and resiliency.

To Practice

When you encounter an obstacle, take a step back, look at the bigger picture, and explore alternatives.

Tenacity—Questions to Ask Yourself

- What is my passion? Do I explore enough to find out?
- How resilient am I? What can I do to increase my resiliency?
- Do I understand the many ways I can achieve my goal?

Notes

1. Sally French, "The Many Failures of Elon Musk, Captured in One Giant Infographic," *Market Watch*, December 12, 2017, accessed June 10, 2021, https://www.marketwatch.com/story/the-many-failures-of-elon-musk-captured-in-one-giant-infographic-2017-05-24.

2. "Messenger RNA (mRNA)," National Human Genome Research Institute, accessed October 2, 2021, https://www.genome.gov/genetics-glossary/messenger-rna.

3. Gina Kolata, "Kati Kariko Helped Shield the World from the Coronavirus," *The New York Times*, April 8, 2021, updated April 17, 2021, accessed June 10, 2021, https://www.nytimes.com/2021/04/08/health/coronavirus-mrna-kariko.html.

4. Damian Garde & Jonathan Saltzman, "The Story of mRNA: How a Once-Dismissed Idea Became a Leading Technology in the Covid Vaccine Race," *Boston Globe*, November 10, 2020, accessed June 10, 2021, https://www.statnews.com/2020/11/10/the-story-of-mrna-how-a-once-dismissed-idea-became-a-leading-technology-in-the-covid-vaccine-race/.

5. David J. Langer, Twitter, November 29, 2020, accessed June 10, 2021, https://twitter.com/drdavidlanger/status/1333218993449086978.

6. Safi Bahcall, *Loonshots: How to Nurture the Crazy Ideas that Win Wars, Cure Diseases, and Transform Industries* (St. Martin's Press, March 19, 2019).

7. Goran Blazeski, "The Story of William Wrigley Jr.—Soap Salesman Who Became the World's Best Gum Manufacturer," *The Vintage News*, November 28, 2016, accessed July 6, 2021, https://www.thevintagenews.com/2016/11/28/the-story-of-william-wrigley-jr-soap-salesman-who-became-the-worlds-best-gum-manufacturer/.

8. Angela Lee Duckworth, "Grit: The Power of Passion and Perseverance," *TED Talks Education*, April 2013, accessed June 10, 2021, https://www.ted.com/talks/angela_lee_duckworth_grit_the_power_of_passion_and_perseverance.

9. "Grit," Merriam-Webster, accessed June 10, 2021, https://www.merriam-webster.com/dictionary/grit.

10. Carol S. Dweck, *Mindset: The New Psychology of Success* (Ballantine Books, December 26, 2007).

11. Lisa Brunette, "Meditation Produces Positive Changes in the Brain," *University of Wisconsin News*, February 6, 2003, accessed October 5, 2021, https://news.wisc.edu/meditation-produces-positive-changes-in-the-brain/.

12. Maria Konnikova, "How People Learn to Become Resilient," February 11, 2016, accessed June 10, 2021, https://www.newyorker.com/science/maria-konnikova/the-secret-formula-for-resilience.

Resources

Angela Lee Duckworth, *Grit: The Power of Passion and Perseverance* (Scribner Book Company, 2016).

Carol S. Dweck, *Mindset: The New Psychology of Success* (Ballantine Books, 2007).

Danny Penman & Mark Williams, *Mindfulness: An Eight-Week Plan for Finding Peace in a Frantic World* (Rodale Books, 2012).

Chapter 4

Get Back

When I hear the song "Get Back," I am reminded
of how curious I was as a child. Getting back to
the way we were as children, full of curiosity and
wonder, can help leaders in many situations. The
words tell me to see problems with an open mind,
ask questions, and be the leader who wants to listen and learn. As a leader, you will encounter many
complex issues. How should you address them? Start
with questions. Get back to that time in your life to
develop a habit of asking questions. This chapter
explores types of problems and ways to use probing
questions to find solutions for them.

About the Song

The Beatles recorded "Get Back" in January 1969
and released it in April of the same year. The *Beatles
Bible*[1] says, "The song began as a satirical and critical

DOI: 10.4324/9781003267546-5   **47**

look at attitudes towards immigrants in Britain. Paul McCartney intended to parody the negative attitudes that were prevalent among politicians and the press." I don't dwell on all the negative connotations when I hear this song. I only know that I need to get back to having a child's perspective, curious to understand and solve problems.

Get Back to Curiosity

I would rather ask a question and be a fool for a moment than remain silent and be a fool for life.

In 2017, headlines buzzed about how a human error caused the outage of Amazon Web Services (AWS) and what Amazon was doing to address it. *The Wall Street Journal* report mentioned[2] that the cost of the service interruption to the 500 largest publicly traded US companies was $150 million based on findings from a company that estimates cyber risks. It also reported that more than half the top 100 e-commerce vendors saw the performance of their sites slow down considerably. Apparently, the outage resulted from the actions of an employee who was trying to improve the performance of the AWS cloud storage billing system. While doing so, by issuing an unintended command, he caused more servers to go offline. That had a cascading effect affecting services to several customers. It also took a long time to restart the servers, resulting in a slow recovery.

Amazon published the reasons and remedies in "Summary of the Amazon S3 Service Disruption in the Northern Virginia (US-EAST-1) Region."[3] The initial diagnosis was that it was because of human error. However, we expect systems such as AWS to be fault-tolerant. We expect them to safeguard against such errors. Training programmers or hiring better programmers are not the answers to this problem. Humans are error-prone. Understanding how to prevent what happened required the AWS engineers to be curious.

Decision-Making Requires Being Curious

Let's look at a decision-making scenario. I am on the board of my undergraduate alumni association. We receive a lot of requests for funds from alumni for various causes. There is always one more request to fund a building. We have a hard time ranking these requests. How do we know where we can make the most impact for the students? We decided to ask about the students' opinions. What areas do they feel need improvements? Are they happy with the curriculum? Do they have good internet connectivity on campus? Do they have a good placement service? Are the students in need of better personal counseling? For the first time in the college's history, the alumni conducted a survey to get the students' input. The analysis of the response provided us with some key areas to focus on. A complicated situation now had some clarity. Armed with this knowledge, we could create initiatives to engage the alumni and the college's administration to make things better at our alma mater.

Complex problems confront world leaders every day. How should you deal with the climate crisis? What strategies can eradicate poverty? How should you address gender inequality? What should you do to educate every child? How should you address homelessness? And more recently, how should you contain the COVID-19 pandemic? We call these complex problems "wicked." Socioeconomic issues are wicked and don't have a definite solution. However, as a society, we can't stop working on them. Being curious is fundamental to our efforts to solve them.

All of the leadership responsibilities require that you ask questions if you want to be an outstanding leader. Asking questions leads to better decision-making. On the AWS problem, the engineering team had to dig deeper to find the solution. They needed to consider more than the superficial answer that human error was the culprit. How does a leader decide when faced with problems? Start by asking questions.

Curiosity Leads to Success

Creativity that leads to ideas is all about asking questions, including questioning the status quo. There have been many stories about how Netflix came to be. According to the founder Reed Hastings, a math problem about the capacity of a station wagon carrying tapes was the spark.[4] Hastings says this led to his question of how much data a DVD could hold, how quickly you can send that information through regular mail, and his anticipation that the internet could make it much faster (streaming). Airbnb is a company that provides a platform for connecting those who have places to rent and travelers who are looking for homes to stay as paying guests. It got started when the founders posed a question—Why should anyone be stranded without a place to stay when we can rent them an air mattress in our house?

What about our fundamental need to connect and network? Breaking the ice requires asking questions such as "What brings you to this event?" Or, when we meet each other, "How are you? How is your family?" In a 2017 study,[5] the researchers found that asking a question, and following up with two more questions, substantially increases the likelihood of you being liked.

In a Knowledge@Wharton leadership interview,[6] *New York Times* editor, Adam Bryant, says he identified two qualities of successful leaders who kept getting promoted throughout their careers—one, passion and curiosity, and two, the ability to have persevered in the face of adversity. He says highly successful leaders are those with inquiring minds. They question everything they see and ask themselves how things work, what makes people tick, and how to make it better.

Think Back to When You Were a Kid

Warren Burger, the author of *The Book of Beautiful Questions* is also the author of *Beautiful Questions in the Classroom*. In a blog post related to this book,[7] he discusses the behavior of kids and adults. Kids ask questions constantly. But they stop asking questions when they grow old. When he discussed this with the creator of the TED Conference, Richard

Saul Wurman, he got an immediate answer—the educational system. The school system rewards them for having answers and not for asking questions. As they progress through school, they ask fewer and fewer questions. Soon they forget the art of questioning (Figure 4.1).

As adults, we are afraid to ask questions for fear that we would be perceived as ignorant. We have to work on overcoming this fear. The ability to ask questions is fundamental to leadership, which also means getting back to our childhood. Children are always asking, "Why?" Being curious helps them learn. We are all born with the innate desire to learn. As children, our desire for knowledge manifests in the many questions we ask our parents, our teachers, and other adults.

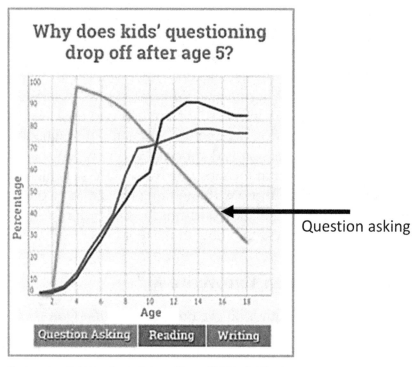

Chart courtesy: Right Question Institute and Berger, W. "Why do kids ask so many questions—and why do they stop?"

Figure 4.1 Questions drop off when we grow.

Building Your Curiosity

In "Are You a Beautiful Questioner?"[8] Warren says:

> *The challenge, then, for adults who want to become better questioners, is to release your inner 4-year-old—that fearless and imaginative questioner we all used to be.*

He asks us to consider the five questions:

"1. Am I willing to be seen as naive?
2. Am I comfortable raising questions with no immediate answers?
3. Am I willing to move away from what I know?
4. Am I open to admitting I might be wrong?
5. Am I willing to slow down and consider?"

These five questions are fundamental to getting back to the state of mind you had when you were a child.

The Five-Whys

We have several ways to solve complicated problems, such as the previously mentioned AWS failure. The goal in many problem-solving situations is to find the root cause and fix it. "5-Whys" is a tool that is very useful in finding the root cause. Sakichi Toyoda, a Japanese industrialist, is credited with developing it. This tool is used in the Toyota Motor Corporation as part of its manufacturing methodologies. It is a technique to find the underlying causes of a problem. Once you find the root cause, you can then create a solution.

The AWS example would trigger the following "5-Whys" process (Figure 4.2).

Problem and causes	Question
Many companies could not service their customers on the internet.	Why couldn't they service the customers ?
Amazon Web Services (AWS) was down.	Why was AWS down?
An engineer tried to debug the S3 system.	Why was the engineer debugging the system?
The system was running slow.	Why did the engineer's action bring the system down?
The system expectations of being able to remove and replace capacity was not met.	Why was the expectation not met?
Safeguards were not in place to prevent debugging action to precipitate massive capacity removal.	*Solution: Add safety checks to prevent such occurrences of debugging actions. Simulation of failure (Disaster Recovery) to implement safeguards to prevent such future failures.*

Figure 4.2 **"5-Whys" process for the AWS problem.**

Complex Problems

Most problems you encounter can be complicated, or we would have already solved them. However, the really tricky ones can be "wicked" complex. The "wicked" complex problems have way too many unknown interrelated parameters, and an algorithm will not solve them.

"5-Whys" is a very effective way to solve merely complicated problems. However, it is not ideal for solving complex problems. The method follows only one train of thought. However, if you use the "5-Whys" multiple times on the same problem, you would be closer to addressing a complex issue.

While not all problems are wicked-complex, we should consider the extreme to learn how to address them. Critical leadership skills such as design thinking, systems thinking, computational thinking, and emotional intelligence can help because each of these skills has curiosity as a fundamental component (Figure 4.3).

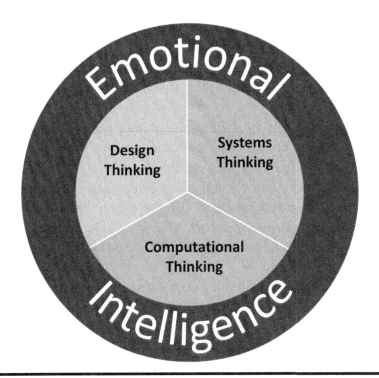

Figure 4.3   Critical skills to solve complex problems.

Design Thinking

Design thinking is an iterative process for building solutions that incorporate curiosity and the art of questioning at every stage. Empathy, a key emotional intelligence component, is fundamental to this process. The organization "Rare" works for environmental change by helping communities in over 60 countries change their behaviors to promote sustainability. It collaborated with Stanford University's design school (called "d.school") to tackle a critical problem facing onion farmers while addressing environment preservation. They wanted to minimize the impact on the already damaged environment by using fewer chemicals.

Instead of asking "Can we reduce the chemicals?" they asked different questions:

- What can communities do to understand their environment?
- How can we empower communities with the right data-driven tools to manage their resources?

The project hopes to find answers to these questions using design thinking. They expect to come up with tools for the local farmers to manage their environment.

Design thinking allows you to go beyond the superficial answers to a complex problem. It helps you to dig deep to understand the problem context. Once you do, you can fashion a bespoke, sustainable solution that considers the context and the stakeholders.

Design thinking challenges your preconceptions, the automatic solution responses that may not be relevant anymore. We no longer have computers with floppy disk drives or mobile phones with physical keyboards, while physical computer keyboards persist. For the longest time, we considered the former features as inviolate as the latter. Design thinking ultimately resulted in their demise.

Systems Thinking

A system is an entity made up of components that depend on and interact with each other. You could say systems thinking is a mindset or a philosophy—a combination of awareness and skills. When we alter one component, the entire system and the other components also change, creating complexity in solving issues in the system. There are many tools available to systems thinkers. The iceberg model is one such tool. Just like an iceberg, which has only a tiny part of it visible above the water, we start with the symptoms. We go down deeper into multiple levels involving patterns and trends, underlying structures, and mental models to get a broad understanding of the challenge.

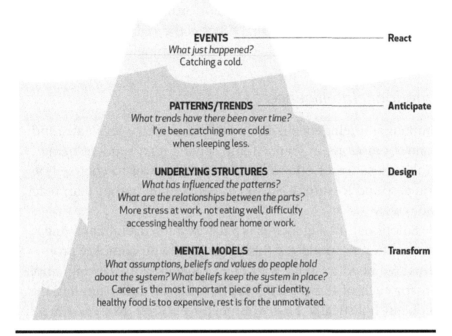

THE ICEBERG
A Tool for Guiding Systemic Thinking

EVENTS ———————————— React
What just happened?
Catching a cold.

PATTERNS/TRENDS ——————— Anticipate
What trends have there been over time?
I've been catching more colds
when sleeping less.

UNDERLYING STRUCTURES ———— Design
What has influenced the patterns?
What are the relationships between the parts?
More stress at work, not eating well, difficulty
accessing healthy food near home or work.

MENTAL MODELS ——————— Transform
What assumptions, beliefs and values do people hold
about the system? What beliefs keep the system in place?
Career is the most important piece of our identity,
healthy food is too expensive, rest is for the unmotivated.

Figure 4.4   Iceberg model to analyze catching cold. (Image courtesy of Ecochallenge.org.)

Figure 4.4 shows an iceberg model applied to an instance of catching a cold.[9]

Computational Thinking

Computational thinking[10] is a thought process involved in solving complex problems, whose key elements are decomposition, pattern recognition, abstraction, and algorithms. Decomposition is a technique to break the problem into manageable parts. Pattern recognition is about finding similarities among these parts. Abstraction helps us ignore unimportant characteristics so that we can focus on relevant information. Algorithms are prescriptions for addressing challenges step by step.

Computational thinking requires you to be curious and ask questions to arrive at a solution. For example, with decomposition, one would have to ask, "What is the right level of decomposition?" Too many levels could be meaningless.

Emotional Intelligence

Emotional intelligence is the ability to perceive, evaluate, and control emotions in yourself and others. As a sentient being in the presence of others, you have the power to choose how you respond to stimuli. Respond deliberately rather than react reflexively.

Emotional intelligence is a must for effectively managing these different modes of thinking. In solving complex problems, we need to work with many stakeholders. Having empathy for each of these stakeholders is key to understanding the problem holistically. First, you need to be self-aware. Asking yourself questions such as: "What am I good at?"; "How can I build my resilience?"; or "How does my team view me as a leader?" helps you become self-aware. Empathizing begins with being curious about the individual and their circumstances. Questions such as "What is your current situation" or "What are your criteria for success of this solution?" are critical to addressing challenges.

How Do You Get Better at Asking Questions?

Just like with other skills, practice helps. You get better at asking questions by asking more questions. When you want to understand complex problems, ask open-ended questions. Think about the multiple-choice questions you get in an exam and an essay question on the same subject. With multiple-choice, you are given three or four answers and asked to pick the right one.

The choices impose a limit on what you can say. Contrast this with an essay question that gives you a problem and asks you for a recommendation to solve it. An example is asking respondents to choose from a list of answers to reduce pollution. When posed as an open-ended question, "How can we reduce pollution?" the respondents would have to reflect on it, analyze all scenarios, and come to a conclusion before answering.

While questions can help bring about a complete definition of a complex problem, you need the right set of people to ask these questions. These are people in your team, your peers, and the stakeholders. Each of them will view the problem through a different lens. Providing a safe space for the team to voice their inputs promotes collective problem-solving. When solving problems, doing your homework is critical. Present what you have learned as the first step to asking more questions—are my facts correct, what am I missing, what should I be asking.

Finally, asking questions is not sufficient. Listen to the answers and act on them. There is nothing worse than raising questions and not following up. When your teams see the results of answering your questions, they get the confidence to speak up and engage with you.

Be a Curious Leader

As a leader, you would want to be able to work out complex problems. You get good at it by being curious. The more questions you ask, the more you become knowledgeable about dealing with complexity. In addition to solving issues, questions also connect you with your team members, who open up to you and share in the decision-making process. Instill a team culture of curiosity. "Get back" to being a curious kid. Success is sure to follow.

Richard Feynman, the Nobel Prize-winning physicist, discussed his now-famous "Ode to a Flower" in a 1981 BBC interview.[11] Feynman says an artist sees a flower and is excited about its beauty. A scientist can also appreciate it. But she goes much deeper than the superficial beauty and starts questioning the purpose of the color of the flower, its structure, and more. When you give yourself the freedom to be curious and dig deeper, you then can conceive of a beauty that goes beyond the surface.

Your responsibility is to encourage your team to appreciate the beauty of the multilayered perspectives that can yield exciting questions, unexpected results, and serendipitous discovery.

Practice

- Next time you encounter a complicated situation that needs resolution, step back and apply the "5-Whys."
- Explore how you can solve a complex problem, even if only a theoretical exercise.

Curiosity—Questions to Ask Yourself

- When I meet someone for the first time, am I curious to know about them? Am I interested only in talking about myself?
- When faced with a problem, do I step back and ask how can I approach the problem?
- When someone comes to me with a problem, how do I react? Do I help them ask questions so that they can help themselves?

Notes

1. "Get Back," The Beatles Bible, accessed October 20, 2021, https://www.beatlesbible.com/songs/get-back/.

2. Laura Stevens, "Amazon Finds the Cause of Its AWS Outage: A Typo," *The Wall Street Journal*, March 2, 2017, accessed June 11, 2021, https://www.wsj.com/articles/amazon-finds-the-cause-of-its-aws-outage-a-typo-1488490506.

3. Amazon Web Services (AWS), "Summary of the Amazon S3 Service Disruption in the Northern Virginia (US-EAST-1) Region," 2017, accessed June 11, 2021, https://aws.amazon.com/message/41926/.

4. Arjun Kharpal, "How a Classic Math Problem Gave Reed Hastings the Idea for Netflix," *CNBC*, February 27, 2017, accessed June 11, 2021, https://www.cnbc.com/2017/02/27/netflix-ceo-reed-hastings-founding-story-became-a-60-billion-firm-inspired-by-a-classic-math-problem.html.

5. Karen Huang, et al., "It Doesn't Hurt to Ask: Question-Asking Increases Liking," *Journal of Personality and Social Psychology*, Vol. 113, No. 3 (2017): 430–452.

6. Interview, "'The Corner Office': Adam Bryant on the Five Qualities of Successful Leaders," *Knowledge@Wharton*, December 17, 2012, accessed June 11, 2021, https://knowledge.wharton.upenn.edu/article/the-corner-office-adam-bryant-on-the-five-qualities-of-successful-leaders/.

7. Warren Berger, "Why Do Kids Ask So Many Questions—And Why Do They Stop?" accessed July 3, 2021, https://amorebeautifulquestion.com/why-do-kids-ask-so-many-questions-but-more-importantly-why-do-they-stop/.

8. Warren Berger, "Are You a Beautiful Questioner?" accessed July 3, 2021, https://www.psychologytoday.com/us/blog/the-questionologist/201806/are-you-beautiful-questioner.

9. Ecochallenge.org, "A Systems Thinking Model: The Iceberg," accessed June 11, 2021, https://ecochallenge.org/iceberg-model/.

10. Jeannette M. Wing, "Computational Thinking," *Communications of the ACM*, Vol. 49, No. 3 (March 2006), also available online, accessed July 22, 2021, http://www.cs.cmu.edu/~wing/publications/Wing06.pdf.

11. From the BBC Interview for Horizon, "The Pleasure of Finding Things Out" (bbc.co.uk/sn/tvradio/programmes/horizon/broadband/archive/feynman/), animated by Fraser Davidson (sweetcrude.tv), accessed August 3, 2021, https://youtu.be/VSG9q_YKZLI.

Resources

Daniel Goleman, *Emotional Intelligence: Why It Can Matter More Than IQ* (Random House Publishing Group, 2005).

Donella Meadows, *Thinking in Systems* (Chelsea Green Publishing, 2008).

Kate Murphy, *You're Not Listening: What You're Missing and Why It Matters* (Celadon Books, 2020).

Warren Berger, *The Book of Beautiful Questions* (Bloomsbury Publishing, 2018).

Chapter 5

Help!

Help! This one-word title reminds me that even leaders need help. Many leaders are hesitant to ask for help because they don't want to look weak. Asking for help and being vulnerable shows the willingness to accept that we don't know all the answers. By asking for support, we signal to others that we are happy to reciprocate and help them. Leaders who show vulnerability invite everyone to contribute. They make collaboration possible, and there is a tremendous benefit to having diverse opinions. Mentors can help leaders when they need advice. Getting help starts with offering to help others. This chapter discusses how to develop the vulnerability to ask for help and a 360-degree feedback tool to understand your blind spots and become a better leader.

DOI: 10.4324/9781003267546-6

About the Song

"Help!" was released as a single in the United States on July 19, 1965, and in the United Kingdom on July 23, 1965, two weeks ahead of the album of the same name. It topped the charts on both sides of the Atlantic.[1] "Help!" was the title song for the second Beatles film of the same name and its soundtrack. Written primarily by John, it was a chart-topper in both the United Kingdom and the United States. He said it manifested a cry for help in the turbulent times of the band members' relationship. Paul's contribution to the song is the countermelody.

Rolling Stone magazine's list of "500 greatest songs of all time" ranked it at 29.

Help!—Being Vulnerable

Are you courageous enough to ask for help?

We have been there—looking back at our lives and wondering what happened to all the simple pleasures in life. As you take on more and more leadership responsibilities, everyone expects you to come up with answers. You feel the need to confide in your best friend or spouse that you are over your head. Yet, you refuse to ask for help from those who can help you: the team members, colleagues, advisors, and mentors. Could it be because you don't like your vulnerability exposed to those you lead? Do you know asking for help is perfectly okay? The world has become more complex in recent times. As a leader, you need to collaborate with others to solve challenging problems that require diverse thoughts.

Being Vulnerable Is Being Courageous

"Vulnerability" was not a word in the list of leadership attributes until recently. Merriam-Webster[2] defines vulnerability as "capable of being physically or emotionally wounded." As a leader, you shy away from this definition. You don't want to be vulnerable, but project an image of strength. But being vulnerable is part of being a human. Sometimes all of us need help.

Brené Brown[3] is the author of five number 1 *New York Times* bestsellers. She spent the past two decades studying courage, vulnerability, shame, and empathy. In her book, *Rising Strong*,[4] Brown says that you judge others who seek your help when you are hard on yourself for needing help. You can't be a good helper when you feel ashamed to ask for help for yourself. Giving and asking for help is using compassion and courage.

Outstanding leaders encourage failures and being vulnerable. One such sports leader is Bruce Bochy, the San Francisco Giant's manager, whose teams won several World Series championships. Bochy has received much praise for his communication skills and humility. Hunter Pence, a four-time All-Star, was a member of the 2012 and 2014 World Series championship teams with the Giants. The story[5] told by Hunter Pence when he joined the Giants celebrates Bochy's leadership that encouraged failures. He explained how Bochy used film clips of an auto race to encourage failing. The clips showed drivers attempting the race repeatedly instead of giving up, even though they were afraid. After seeing these clips, Pence felt it was okay to fail for the first time. He learned that you have to keep going even when you mess up. There is no shame in failure. Pence said the message "step on the gas" was inspirational.

In the 1990s, as a director of engineering, I led several software engineering teams. With their help, I delivered multiple releases of software solutions with quality and on schedule. But I never realized how some of my team members, peers, and superiors viewed me. In one of my performance reviews, my manager said if I wanted to grow as a leader, I should get some coaching. I signed up for leadership training with a personal coach. She said she has a proven method of helping leaders. The first step was to get a 360-degree assessment from my colleagues. This assessment gets feedback on your performance from your peers, team members, and supervisors. I could choose those who can give me this assessment. A self-assessment is also part of this. Using this feedback, we identified the areas of improvement. When the results came back, the coach sat down with me and went over the good and the bad. The feedback said I had two areas I needed to improve to become a better leader: I was too defensive when receiving criticism and too hard on myself and my team members.

I felt awful hearing this feedback. However, I realized that if I want to grow as a leader, I must address these shortcomings. I embraced the opportunity to be coached and started being mindful of my interactions. I changed my behavior—one of the best decisions I made. I came out of the coaching experience willing to be open and grow.

Over the years I have been leading, I came to realize that all of us are vulnerable. However, we choose to manifest our vulnerability in different ways. In my case, I manifested it by being defensive, closed, and responding negatively. It would have been better to ask how I could make it better. That would have been courageous. Luckily, I learned to do just that with the 360-degree feedback and changing my behavior. You can do that too.

Mentoring and Help

One of my greatest joys comes from mentoring. There is nothing more uplifting than when someone reaches out to you and asks for help or advice. You feel exhilarated when hearing "Can you help me?" or, "What do you think?" I have mentored hundreds of people, and some were on my global engineering teams. There are college students from my undergraduate alma mater who are my mentees. A few of them are from professional societies such as the Society of Women Engineers. No matter where they come from, all of them overcame their fears and embraced vulnerability to ask for help. They implicitly tell me they trust me, my judgment, opinions, and recommendations. I am honored every time someone asks me to mentor them. Whenever I hesitate to ask for help, I bring up in my mind a picture of all of my mentees, and then I am not afraid to be open and courageous. You can do something similar by imagining those who asked you for help.

Organizations Need Help Too!

Leaders are aware of the capabilities of their teams and their limitations and seek the help of experts in the field for guidance, but, ultimately, they own the outcome. In today's complex situations, getting external advice is not unusual. Technology has made a lot of business practices obsolete. Take the case of Walmart, the retail leader. Amazon and e-commerce disrupted their business. The leaders of Walmart acknowledged they needed help and sought this help in multiple ways. Walmart acquired the eCommerce vendor Jet.com, whose founder Marc Lore became the head of e-commerce operations. They set up shop in the heart of Silicon Valley, the technology innovation hub, and grew their technical capabilities. In India, one of the fastest-growing economies, they invested in Flipkart. Their efforts seem to pay off. They are now a formidable competitor to Amazon.

How Do You Get Help?

A critical component of your growth in the leadership journey is getting help. Many leaders are afraid to ask for help. They worry about giving the impression of being incompetent. They fear that help won't be forthcoming. If you can overcome this fear, you can become a successful leader. Helping others is the first step in getting help for yourself.

Giving Help Is Key to Getting Help

It's challenging to give help, and some people will misinterpret that as your lack of confidence in them. Others might be suspicious about the ulterior motive behind your offer. Make sure they desire help. If you are aware of the specifics, you can assess your ability to help. Ask for details. Pose the question in such a way that shows you are not gaining anything by giving help. Then, those who receive the question will open up to you. If stated with sincerity, this question signals you are open, willing, approachable, and trustable. Even when you cannot help someone yourself, recommending someone who can help generates so much goodwill.

Build reciprocal and durable relationships. When someone you helped endorses you, your standing as a leader goes up, which can help you be vulnerable. An effective leader looks to her teams and empowers those who can help. Others' capabilities do not threaten her. She shares authority, praises the team member who came up with an idea, doesn't steal the limelight, attributes successes to the team, but owns the failures. She has mutual respect and trust with the team members. Asking for the help of a subordinate may seem like acknowledging a shortcoming. You expect a leader to be strong, projecting competence. But it does not mean you know everything. Competency means being decisive after considering all the facts.

An Example of a Vulnerable Leader—Peer Help

Help from peers is essential to leading. Let me explain this using the role of a product manager, rather than the obvious one, that of a CEO (Figure 5.1). The product manager's job is very much like that of a CEO. She must possess sufficient knowledge to interact with the stakeholders. She needs their help. Finance needs to provide input to the decisions on cost and budget, and legal assistance is required with the privacy issues of the product. She needs to get help from engineering in determining the schedule and features. Input from operations is required on service levels and the trade-offs involved in determining price. She needs to elicit sales targets. Marketing has to collaborate

Figure 5.1 Product manager and stakeholders.

with her on product launch and collateral. She also needs
to interact with the most important stakeholder, the customer. They provide her valuable input on the product.
Given this, no wonder that a product manager is a critical
resource in an organization. The successful product leaders
have the vulnerability to approach all her stakeholders and
ask for their help in performing her role. When you lack
the courage to ask for help, imagine the role of a product
manager.

Help from the Frontline, Peers, and a Growth Mindset

As you move up the career ladder, you will delegate the details to those in your team and get their help in making sound decisions. You don't have to solve all the problems by yourself. Your success will come from being able to harness the capabilities of everyone in your team. I accepted that the technical leaders have more knowledge of a specific technology than I did in my engineering organization. I removed their obstacles to achieving excellence. They helped me make the right decision in selecting a technology or vendor. Two things happen when you do this. First, you gain the trust of your team. Second, your team becomes empowered to achieve the common goals and is motivated to contribute. Nothing makes the team happier than the realization that they helped make the right decision.

Before asking for help, do your homework. Understand where you need help. Today, with all the search tools available on the internet, you can find tons of information on any subject. Read, or watch videos, to understand some basics. State your understanding when asking for help, and then seek suggestions on the subject. You come across as credible when you do this. We often like to help those who help themselves. When you get conflicting input, a brainstorming session can resolve them.

To reiterate, the traditional interaction of a leader and follower is one that appears to suggest the leader has all the answers and can guide the follower. However, a wise leader knows she doesn't have all the answers. Comprehending this is the difference between being a leader who is growing and one who stands still. Successful leaders cultivate a growth mindset as opposed to having a fixed mindset (Figure 5.2). A fixed mindset belongs to a static entity, shrinking away from challenges, avoiding constructive criticism, and viewing the

Fixed Mindset
- Avoid Challenges
- Give up when facing obstacles
- Look at efforts as a waste of time
- Defensive when faced with criticism
- Belittle or feel threatened by others' successes

Growth Mindset
- Embrace Challenges
- Persist
- Look at efforts as building expertise
- Welcome constructive criticism
- Celebrate and learn from others' successes

Figure 5.2   Mindsets.

success of others as a failure. A growth mindset is when you believe you are growing all the time, learning, and developing. It helps you embrace challenges and invite and act on constructive criticism. With an expanding mind, you celebrate the success of others as something to be learned from and use that as inspiration.

360-Degree Assessment: A Tool to Determine Where You Need Help

Use a 360-degree assessment[6] to understand the areas where you need help (Figure 5.3). This assessment stresses the value of external feedback, which is critical when you are not self-aware. Input from more people can help you understand how others perceive your areas of strengths and weaknesses.

As the name implies, the 360-degree assessment is about getting a holistic view of your performance, looking at it from

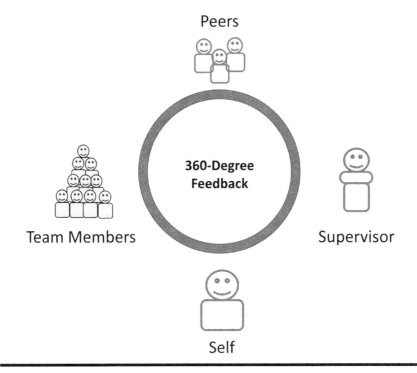

Figure 5.3   360-Degree assessment.

all angles. How do you view yourself? What are your strengths and weaknesses? Does your supervisor have feedback on what she is pleased with, and what are the areas of improvement? How do your team members see you? Do they see some areas that need work? How do your peers evaluate your performance based on your interactions with them? All the feedback is anonymous and confidential, so that everyone can express an honest opinion. When you are getting this assessment, you identify the people whose feedback matters to you. For example, if you have a tough time with a team member, his feedback can be valuable. The assessment questionnaire requires careful consideration. You don't want it to be a platform for gripe. Instructions to the participants should be clear that the feedback must be constructive. The most important aspect of this assessment is follow-through. It would be helpful to create a plan to act on the findings.

If you are leading a customer-facing organization, get feedback from customers as well. If you lead a team that works with partners, get feedback from them.

SurveyMonkey[7] has good tips on how to create good questionnaires, and they also provide a question bank.[8]

Leaders Need Mentoring Too

An effective way to ask for help is by finding a mentor. A study conducted by Suzanne de Janasz and Maury Peiperl[9] about mentoring and CEOs found among the 45 CEOs in the study who had formal mentoring arrangements, 84% credited their mentors with helping them avoid costly mistakes and achieving proficiency faster. Find a mentor to help you. Do your homework. Choose specific areas where you need help and prioritize them. Identify mentors who are proficient in them. You will need to research their proficiency and also verify that they have time to mentor you. Be clear about how long you want to be mentored. Is it short-term or long-term? Is there already a relationship with the mentor through your work or network? If so, you are in good shape. As discussed earlier, if you build relationships long before you need help, asking for help becomes effortless.

An informal way of asking for help is to air your concerns in your leadership network. Perhaps some of them experienced similar challenges and dealt with them.

A Vulnerable Leader Is an Ever-Growing Leader

A vulnerable leader is not afraid to ask for help. By asking for help, you become approachable. Your team members see you fostering collaboration. They gain the confidence to reach out when they need help. Every one of us has room for improvement. Feedback from those we work with can help with that. Have the courage to be a vulnerable leader.

Practice

- Take a 360-degree assessment to identify areas of improvement. Explore how you can get help and follow through.
- The next time you are stumped with a challenge, go through a deliberate process of asking a team member for help.

Vulnerability—Questions to Ask Yourself

- Do I struggle with problems for too long instead of getting help?
- Do I listen to critical feedback to better myself?
- Am I aware of my blind spots?

Notes

1. "Help!" The Beatles Bible, accessed October 20, 2021, https://www.beatlesbible.com/songs/help/.
2. Merriam-Webster Dictionary, "Vulnerable," accessed June 9, 2021, https://www.merriam-webster.com/dictionary/vulnerable.
3. Brené Brown, brenebrown.com, accessed June 10, 2021, https://brenebrown.com/.
4. Brené Brown, *Rising Strong: How the Ability to Reset Transforms the Way We Live, Love, Parent, and Lead* (Random House, April 4, 2017).
5. Jake Montero, "Shortly after Joining Giants, Bruce Bochy Gave Hunter Pence a Message that Changed the Course of His Career," *KNBR.com*, September 24, 2019, accessed July 3, 2021, https://www.knbr.com/2019/09/24/shortly-after-joining-giants-bruce-bochy-gave-hunter-pence-a-message-that-changed-course-of-his-career/.
6. Daniel Goleman & Richard E. Boyatzis, "Emotional Intelligence Has 12 Elements. Which Do You Need to Work on?" February 6, 2017, accessed June 10, 2021, https://hbr.org/2017/02/emotional-intelligence-has-12-elements-which-do-you-need-to-work-on.

7. Survey Monkey, "Writing Good Survey Questions," accessed June 10, 2021, https://www.surveymonkey.com/mp/writing-survey-questions/.

8. Survey Monkey, "Introducing Question Bank," accessed June 10, 2021, https://www.surveymonkey.com/curiosity/question-bank/.

9. Suzanne de Janasz & Maury Peiperl, "CEOs Need Mentors Too," *Harvard Business Review*, Vol. 93 (2015): 100–103, accessed June 10, 2021, https://hbr.org/2015/04/ceos-need-mentors-too.

Resources

Brené Brown, *Dare to Lead* (Vermilion, 2018).
Carol Dweck, *Mindset: The New Psychology of Success* (Ballantine Books, 2007).

Chapter 6

Think for Yourself

"Think for Yourself" reminds me that I must be an independent thinker to be an innovative and authentic leader. It is easy to accept what you read or hear from the past. You need to do substantial work to question the conventional wisdom. But the rewards are significant when you think for yourself. Learn to use the many mental models and apply them to suit the situation. Outstanding leaders are lateral thinkers, and they find connections and relationships not clear today. Reflect on what you read and observe, and connect the dots. Make time for thinking.

About the Song

The song "Think for Yourself" features in the 1965 album called *Rubber Soul*. George Harrison wrote the lyrics, promoting independent thinking. It is conventional to use only one bass guitar part. The Beatles

DOI: 10.4324/9781003267546-7

incorporated two in this song. One of them was a standard bass. Another was music distortion using a device called "fuzzbox." The Beatles were constantly innovating, and their ingenuity in using two basses showcases this.

Think for Yourself

> *Leaders who find time for deep thinking are well rewarded.*

In "On Thinking for Oneself,"[1] Schopenhauer reinforced the message of individual thought. He compared the vast knowledge one may have to an enormous library. A large library that is in disarray is no good compared to a well-organized small library. Similarly, extensive knowledge that is not deep or "thoroughly pondered" is less valuable.

His message is straightforward—when you learn something, chew over it, turn it over in your mind to clearly understand what you learned. Analyze what you learned and create a usable mental model that can be applied to actual life situations. The ability to retrieve such models is essential for solving problems in a crisis.

As leaders, you spend your days solving problems and making decisions. When you ponder a situation, be sure to evaluate different options to deal with it. Organize your thoughts based on previous observations and accumulated wisdom and arrive at a course of action by thinking for yourself. We are aware of the power of independent thinkers like Leonardo da Vinci, Albert Einstein, Benjamin Franklin, and James Watt from history. Business leaders who cultivate independent thinking can achieve brilliant success for themselves and their teams.

As an aspiring leader, you can learn from your supervisors, peers, and other leaders you encounter. There are many valuable lessons to be had. But use these lessons as stepping stones. Add your independent thinking. Have the courage to be true to your convictions.

Personal Narratives

I confess to being a self-help junkie. In recent years, I have expanded my reading to anything that catches my eyes on the internet. Apparently, I am not alone. A 2019 study estimates the market for self-improvement products and services to be over 11 billion dollars.[2] However, I am incredibly picky about what I choose to do with what I learn. I am a unique human being. No one is just like me, while an "average person" is the target of such a market.

For example, self-help books will tell you to start your day early. We all have heard, "Early to bed and early to rise makes a man healthy, wealthy, and wise." Does this work for everybody? Thomas Edison, the legendary inventor, was a late riser. He always worked late into the night and seldom woke up before late morning. Do you know that Winston Churchill, Bob Dylan, Samuel Johnson, Carl Jung, Franz Kafka, and Prince were also late risers? Daily habits support our aspirations. When they do, you don't need to give them up. A leader is aware of conventional wisdom but is not afraid to go against it.

While growing up in India in the 1960s, I was painfully aware of the dowry system. A dowry is a payment that the bride's family makes to the groom's family. I decided not to get married in this conventional way. I used to say I would rather remain single, stuck to my convictions, and wedded someone outside my social class and religion, circumventing the legacy system and asserting my point of view.

Toastmasters is an organization that promotes public speaking. The organization has thousands of clubs in which the members practice their speeches and develop leadership skills. There are three segments in every club meeting. One of them is about prepared speeches. The second one is about impromptu speaking. Evaluations fall in the third segment. Many of the evaluators follow the Toastmasters' conventional wisdom on what creates an impressive speech. Catchy opening? Check. Body movements? Check. Vocal variety? Check. Call to action? Check. I have found that many speakers who compete in Toastmasters follow this formula. After joining

Toastmasters, I wondered if I was wasting my time. I didn't want to be a winning contestant. I just wanted to get my points across without hesitation and with clarity. That meant accepting some of the Toastmasters' recommendations for a winning speech but ignoring others.

Question the Conventional Wisdom

When I wanted to study engineering in the 1960s, I had no role models. I was interested in engineering, and I could not care if conventional wisdom reserved that field for males. My family encouraged my independent reasoning by facilitating my relocation to another city and helped me enroll in a prestigious engineering college. In 2017, when I was researching pioneering engineering women for my book,[3] I came across stories of many women. They were not as lucky as I was in having support for their independent thinking. One of them told me that her ultra-orthodox family fought her every step of the way. They worried she would have a tough time getting married and pulled her out of the engineering college only a few months after she started. She didn't give up and persisted and got her engineering education. She brought innovations to the company where she worked after graduating.

American history has many examples of those who questioned conventional wisdom. The women of suffrage movement asked why women don't have the same rights as men. Rosa Parks refused to give up her seat on a bus to a white man. Without them questioning conventional wisdom, the lives of women and people of color would be very different today.

Robert Taylor, the creator of Softsoap, looked at the puddle in a soap dish after multiple uses of the soap. Taylor wondered if there could be a way to deliver soap as a liquid that one can pump out of a plastic bottle. He realized anyone could copy his idea. He bought 100 million of the pumps, preventing immediate copycat brands. His innovation made a lot of money before being acquired for $61 million by Colgate-Palmolive.[4]

Make your own trail.

Robert Taylor was a trailblazer. He also made sure he had a head start protecting his business.

Listen to Your Inner Voice

Leaders often find themselves in situations where their inner voice tells them to do something against others' advice or know that doing so would not be popular. The courage of conviction to listen to your inner voice and act on it is a hallmark of an exceptional leader. In the chapter on using your intuition, I discuss how it helps leaders in decision-making when there is not enough data to use analytical methods. There are many examples in history where courageous individuals acted on their inner voices and kept pressing on despite all the failures they encountered. Recently, Jeff Bezos tweeted about a *Barron's* magazine article from 1999 which predicted the death of Amazon.com[5] and offered the advice that while you should be open to suggestions and information, don't let anyone tell you who you are. One can imagine how such articles made him more determined to succeed.

Find your inner voice and develop your passion and influence those around you to be their best.

Learning to Be an Independent Thinker

Innovative leaders are not afraid of going against conventional wisdom. An expression in the information technology industry used to be "Nobody ever got fired for buying IBM." Conventional wisdom is a safe path but a lazy one. Thinking for oneself requires work. It is much easier to go with what you see superficially from the source of information. The question "Why?" is the guiding light in doing the hard work of asserting the truth for oneself.

Your first step is to become self-aware. You should understand your feelings, motives, and personal aspirations. Jeff Weiner[6] advocates being in the moment and mindful practices to achieve it in his LinkedIn Leadership course. When you are self-aware, thinking becomes self-directed. You selectively apply what you learned through books, the opinions of others, and what you read on social media.

As a leader, you direct your thinking to solve a problem. You expect your contemplations to result in concrete action. In "How to Think for Yourself,"[7] author and computer programmer, Scott Young, proposes that thinking and learning are two sides of the same coin. I believe this is true. Thinking for oneself doesn't mean you ignore the information that is already available to you. To think for yourself, you should be informed and question what you know. Understand the existing wisdom, so you can judge for yourself to propose an alternative thesis or find a novel way to solve problems.

Put your thoughts into action. What you learn from it then strengthens your thoughts. It becomes a virtuous cycle of thinking and doing (Figure 6.1).

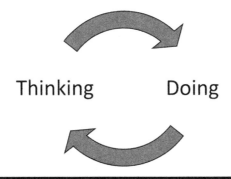

Thinking   Doing

Figure 6.1   Thinking–doing.

Your Team and Thinking for Oneself

Members of your team should also think for themselves. The first step in achieving this is to trust them. Trust builds confidence, and confidence gives the freedom to express independent thoughts. Encourage your team by empowering them. Autonomy over their creative decisions prepares the team to defend themselves when questioned. They would be well prepared because they have thought their ideas through (Figure 6.2).

When your team member comes to you for direction or advice on a topic, ask her what she thinks about it. As she expresses her thoughts, gently guide her, collaborate, and let her arrive at answers. You have heard the timeless adage, "Give a man a fish, and you feed him for a day. Teach a man to fish, and you feed him for a lifetime." By adopting a coaching leadership style when appropriate, you can help your team to think for themselves. They will then grow intellectually and become leaders themselves. Reinforce the behavior with rewards. A leader who promotes individual thought promotes a culture of innovation, curiosity, and initiatives.

Thinking Frameworks—Mental Models

Mental models help you think better. They represent how things work and help us make sense of the complex

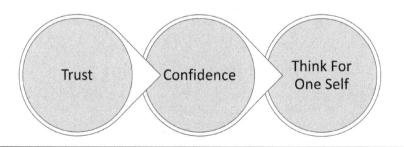

Figure 6.2 Team thinking.

situations we encounter. They assist us in sifting through the vast array of information we gather from different sources and use them in our problem-solving. There are many of them, and each situation requires we apply an appropriate one.

One of my favorite mental models is the Pareto principle (or the 80/20 rule). This rule states that roughly 80% of consequences come from 20% of causes (the "vital few").[8] The originator of this mental model, Vilfredo Pareto, observed the output of peas in his garden and found that 20% of the peapods resulted in 80% of the peas produced. He developed the macroeconomic principle that 80% of the wealth was in the hands of 20% of the Italian population. In my long career leading product development, I have used this mental model frequently. For example, you can attribute a majority of software bugs to a small set of code. A small percentage of super-productive software engineers handle the bulk of a software release outcome. Twenty percent of the customers contribute 80% of a company's revenue. The Pareto principle helps you decide where to direct your attention to get the best outcome in any situation. The capability of the team goes up when you foster the use of such mental models.

80/20 Rule: An Example

Any software organization has more defects and feature enhancements than what the resources can handle. We have to address the showstoppers. What to do with the rest? How do we prioritize them? In my organization, we used the 80/20 rule. We looked at our customers and the revenue they contribute (Figure 6.3).

We focused on the defects and feature requests from those customers who contributed 80% of the revenue and addressed the rest as the resources would allow.

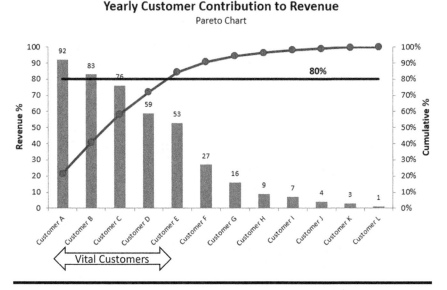

Figure 6.3   Pareto chart—customers and revenue.

An old Indian parable, "The elephant and the blind men," is appropriate in discussing the need for multiple mental models. In this fable, a group of blind men came across an elephant, an animal they know nothing about, and tried to describe it by touching it. Each of them could feel only a part of the elephant (Figure 6.4).

The Need for Multiple Mental Models

One man touched the trunk, and the other the ear, and so on. Each of the men described the elephant in terms of the limited experience they had. The man who felt the trunk said it was a snake. The one who ran his hands over the elephant's ear was sure he was touching a fan. Each had a limited experience, and that resulted in what they thought.

Knowledge from a single discipline limits how you view problems. You see them through a narrow lens. How can you overcome the blindness? It is by applying multiple mental

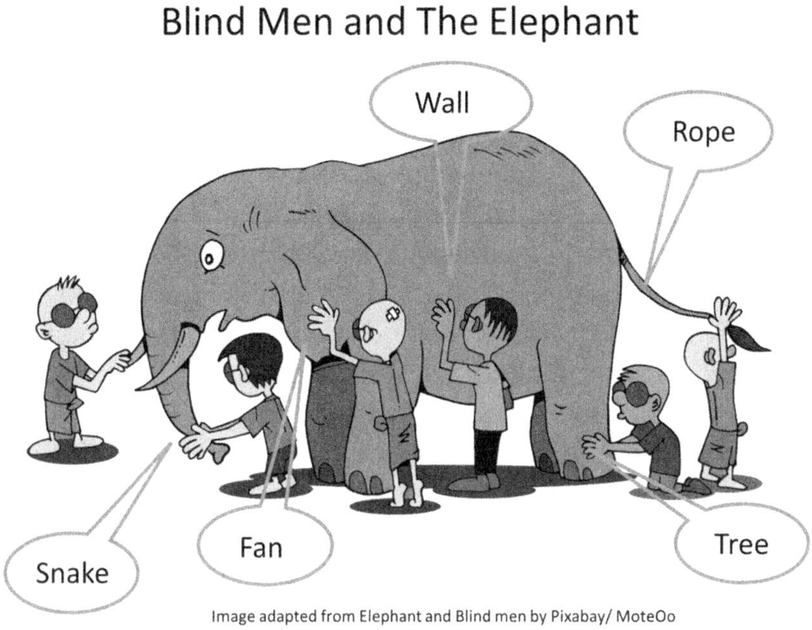

Blind Men and The Elephant

Image adapted from Elephant and Blind men by Pixabay/ MoteOo

Figure 6.4   Blind men and the elephant.

models drawn from several disciplines. They help you with the diversity of thought and help you avoid siloed thinking.

Thinking Frameworks—Lateral Thinking

Edward de Bono, author, physician, and philosopher, coined the term "lateral thinking," which is the opposite of vertical thinking, where you follow a step-by-step process. In lateral thinking, you look at the problem at hand in a novel way to find a solution, often borrowing the learning from another domain. In his book *Lateral Thinking: Creativity Step by Step,*[9] de Bono describes ways to learn lateral thinking, all about changing patterns.

There are two types of thinking, vertical and lateral. Vertical thinking is sequential and applies an existing design to a situation. Lateral thinking looks at the pattern and tries to change its structure. It does that by reorganizing the information in multiple ways.

You can restructure a pattern to get a new one. Or you can combine several and create an entirely new one.

Lateral thinking techniques proposed by de Bono include generating alternatives, challenging assumptions, innovation, suspended judgment, fractionation and reassembly, reversal (look at things inside out, upside down), and use of analogies.

"Six Thinking Hats" is a method proposed by de Bono to encourage parallel thinking.[10] In this method, you direct your brain to think in six distinct directions—big picture and managing, facts and information, feelings and emotions, negatives, positives, and new ideas. Then you can consider different aspects of the problem you are facing, think in each direction, and arrive at a solution.

A Lateral Thinking Example from History

The story of James Watt and the steam engine is an excellent illustration of lateral thinking. As a young boy, Watt observed steam lifting the lid of the teakettle in his mother's kitchen. He saw the water condensing back into the kettle. This observation brought forth in his mind later in life would become critical in developing steam engines. Thomas Newcomen was the first to invent a commercially successful steam engine.[11] However, Watt brought the learning from his childhood and came up with an efficient mechanism. His proposed solution involving a separate condenser increased the amount of work per unit of fuel used. Lateral thinking made this revolutionary development possible.

A Lateral Thinking Example from My Start-up

The start-up I cofounded was in a neighborhood where robberies were cropping up. The computer systems we used for our software development were easy targets. When break-ins happened in the middle of the night, the police would call those of us closest to the office. The company couldn't afford a better location, so we came up with an idea to put a prison cell inside the building. The cell was inexpensive and easy to install, and we secured all the computers in it. When the robbers broke into the building, they couldn't get their hands on them. We could sleep at night.

Mind–Body Connection and Time to Think

If you want others to follow, learn to be alone with your thoughts.

—**William Deresiewicz**[12]

The practice of independent thinking requires patience and time.

Several studies on the impact of exercise, including walking, have called out the connection between being active and cognitive functions. In "Keep on Walking,"[13] the author describes how walking has been beneficial. There is anecdotal support for the link between walking and superior thinking. Jeremy DeSilva is an anthropologist at Dartmouth College. In the article "On the Link Between Great Thinking and Obsessive Walking,"[14] he talks about great thinkers such as Charles Darwin, Ralph Waldo Emerson, Henry David Thoreau, John Muir, Jonathan Swift, Immanuel Kant, Beethoven, and Friedrich Nietzsche, and their obsession with walking. Darwin's best place to think was not his study. His contemplation took place on a path he called "Sandwalk," now known as "Darwin's thinking path." He used to go around that path five times, about half a mile. It gave him a routine and gave him time to think.

DeSilva acknowledges that one could conclude that brilliant thinkers were more likely to go for a walk. Note that walking alone for long allows you to be alone with your thoughts, thus giving you ample time to think.

In his 2014 *New Yorker* article "Why Walking Helps Us Think,"[15] Ferris Jabr offers several reasons walking enables us to think better. Walking is an exercise. It increases the blood flow to the brain, helps make new connections between brain cells, and boosts brain activity. Unlike the well-regulated speeds you get on exercise machines or treadmills in a gym, walking synchronizes our mood to the pace. It creates a rhythm that is conducive to thinking and doesn't require any conscious effort. Our brains have all the time to think.

Some studies have established a link between walking and creativity. One such study, conducted by Stanford University researchers,[16] concluded that walking allows ideas to flow freely and helps achieve greater creativity while increasing physical activity.

Think for Yourself

Think for yourself by understanding and questioning conventional wisdom. You will have superior outcomes in your decision-making when you do so and will grow outstanding organizations. Have the courage to stick to your convictions and be authentic. Teach yourself and your team to be independent thinkers using frameworks, such as mental models and lateral thinking. Become better at it by spending time and using the power of mind–body connection.

Practice

- Learn the Mental Models (see resources). Scan the list of mental models to see which one would fit a specific situation/problem. Use the model to address the issue.
- Take long walks and give yourself time to think.
- Solve lateral thinking puzzles.

Think for Yourself—Questions to Ask Yourself

- Do I encourage my team members to think for themselves?
- Do I use diverse thinking in problem-solving?
- What steps am I taking to improve my thinking?

Notes

1. Arthur Schopenhauer, translated by Thomas Bailey Saunders, "The Art of Literature/On Thinking for Oneself," *Wikisource*, January 5, 2021, accessed June 10, 2021, https://en.wikisource .org/wiki/The_Art_of_Literature/On_Thinking_for_Oneself.
2. Marketdata Enterprises, "$11 Billion Self-Improvement Market Is Growing, but Has Its Critics," *WebWire*, October 15, 2019, accessed June 10, 2021, https://www.webwire.com/ ViewPressRel.asp?aId=248507.
3. Shantha Mohan, *Roots and Wings: Inspiring Stories of Indian Women in Engineering* (Notion Press, 2018).
4. Steve Chawkins, "Robert R. Taylor Dies at 77; Entrepreneur Created Softsoap," *Los Angeles Times*, September 11, 2013, accessed June 10, 2021, https://www.latimes.com/local/obituar-ies/la-xpm-2013-sep-11-la-me-robert-taylor-20130912-story.html.
5. Justin Bariso, "Jeff Bezos's Viral Tweet Is Only 38 Words, but It Teaches a Master Class in How to Handle Criticism," *Inc.*, accessed October 25, 2021, https://www.inc.com/justin-bariso/ amazon-jeff-bezos-how-to-deal-with-criticism-how-to-deal-with -negative-feedback-emotional-intelligence-growth-mindset.html.
6. Jeff Weiner, "Three Pillars of Effective Leadership," *LinkedIn Learning*, September 3, 2020, accessed June 10, 2021, https:// www.linkedin.com/learning/on-leadership-by-jeff-weiner.
7. Scott H. Young, "How to Think for Yourself," accessed August 14, 2021, https://www.scotthyoung.com/blog/2021/05/13/think -for-yourself/.
8. "Pareto Principle," Wikipedia, accessed July 23, 2021, https://en .wikipedia.org/wiki/Pareto_principle.
9. Edward de Bono, *Lateral Thinking: Creativity Step by Step* (Harper & Row, 1970).

10. Edward de Bono, *Six Thinking Hats* (Little Brown and Company, 1985).
11. "Steam Engine," Wikipedia, July 7, 2021, accessed July 18, 2021, https://en.wikipedia.org/wiki/Steam_engine.
12. William Deresiewicz, "Solitude and Leadership," *American Scholar*, March 1, 2010, accessed June 10, 2021, https://theamericanscholar.org/solitude-and-leadership/.
13. Edward M. Wojtys, "Keep on Walking," *Sports Health*, Vol. 7, No. 4 (2015): 297–298, accessed June 10, 2021, https://www.ncbi.nlm.nih.gov/pmc/articles/PMC4481680/.
14. Jeremey DeSilva, "On the Link between Great Thinking and Obsessive Walking," *Literary Hub*, April 19, 2021, accessed June 10, 2021, https://lithub.com/on-the-link-between-great-thinking-and-obsessive-walking/.
15. Ferris Jabr, "Why Walking Helps Us Think," *New Yorker*, September 3, 2014, accessed June 10, 2021, https://www.newyorker.com/tech/annals-of-technology/walking-helps-us-think.
16. Marily Oppezzo & Daniel L. Schwartz, "Give Your Ideas Some Legs: The Positive Effect of Walking on Creative Thinking," *Journal of Experimental Psychology: Learning, Memory, and Cognition*, Vol. 40, No. 4 (2014): 1142–1152, https://doi.org/10.1037/a0036577.

Resources

Charlie T. Munger, *Poor Charlie's Almanack: The Wit and Wisdom of Charles T. Munger* (Walsworth Publishing Company, 2005).
Edward de Bono, *Lateral Thinking: Creativity Step by Step* (Harper & Row, 1970).
Farnam Street, "Reading Better," *fs.blog*, accessed July 27, 2021, https://fs.blog/reading/.
Frans Johansson, *The Medici Effect: What Elephants and Epidemics Can Teach Us about Innovation* (Harvard Business Review Press, 2017).
Roger Martin, *The Opposable Mind* (Harvard Business Review Press, 2009).
Shane Parrish & Rhiannon Beaubien, *The Great Mental Models Volume 1: General Thinking Concepts* (Latticework Publishing Inc., 2019).

LEADERSHIP
SKILLS

2

Chapter 7

I Want to Tell You

Leaders are successful only when they can express their thoughts well. Precise communication is critical for leadership success. It is not enough to know the basics—you must be able to communicate and adapt your style to suit the situation. Today, technological advances have multiplied the means of communication. For remote communications, besides phone calls, you use emails, instant messages, and online meetings. You can also use online venues such as blogs and social media—Twitter, Facebook, LinkedIn, and Instagram. Become proficient in different platforms and channels of communication. We will explore the framework for leadership communication in this chapter.

About the Song

Released in 1966, "I Want to Tell You" appeared on the album *Revolver*, the first time George had three

DOI: 10.4324/9781003267546-9

songs on an album. George spoke about having a flood of thoughts and the difficulty in conveying them, and this song was his way of sharing his inadequacy in communication. This song reminds me we all experience similar challenges. It is essential to overcome them if you want to be impactful in your leadership. I also love the other two songs on the album, "Love You To," incorporating Indian instruments, Sitar and Tabla, and "Taxman."

I Want to Tell You—The Art of Communicating

Leadership communication is conversation.

Think of a leader you like. Is she an excellent communicator? I bet she is. Outstanding leaders differentiate themselves with clear communication. They didn't become good at it overnight. True, some of us are born with the gift of gab. Luckily for the rest of us, there are many tools available to become better at communicating.

Recently, as part of my Toastmasters education, I took the assessment to evaluate my communication style. There are four communication styles—direct, supportive, initiating, and analytical. The result said mine is a direct communication style. What does this mean? A direct communicator is "results-oriented, focused, and competitive." The assessment was not a surprise, which also said, "others may sometimes perceive you as impatient and demanding," probably a good characterization.

Bucketing us into one of these styles is probably simplistic. While the assessment described me as a direct communicator, communication styles are situational, which is supported by the many decades of my software engineering leadership. When I am talking about accomplishing a project or getting a new software release out, I am direct. But when I am talking to a team member about a personal situation, I am an active listener, patient, and sympathetic. I try to be analytical when we discuss a specific technology or process focused on problem-solving. I fall a little short on initiating communication, and this is to do with me being more of an introvert.

Leaders and the Art of Communication

Indra Nooyi, the former CEO of PepsiCo, is an excellent leader who is a situational communicator. She talked about her leadership journey with David Novak, retired chair, and CEO, Yum! Brands on his leadership platform.[1] When Indra took over as the CEO of PepsiCo, she had to create a vision and communicate it to the organization. The communication needed to be inspirational and truthful. Indra wanted to assuage the fears typically present during transitions. She also had to communicate her plans. The organization needed to understand the short-term goals for execution. The long-term goals were essential to keep everyone aligned.

John Chambers is the former CEO and chair of Cisco, who took the company from $1.2 billion in 1995 to $47 billion in 2015. He stepped down as the CEO that year. He is the author (with Diane Brady) of the book *Connecting the Dots: Lessons for Leadership in a Startup World*. Chambers is hailed as a great communicator. In the "Working Capital Conversations Podcast,"[2] he says you cannot be an excellent leader today without strong communication skills. He talks about the speed of doing business in the digitized world of today. Communication strategies need to grow with time. Chambers is a big proponent of listening. He implores leaders to listen to customers, ask questions, and follow up.

In his blog on leadership, author Jacob Morgan talks about the former CEO of Discover Financial, David Nelms.[3] Communication has evolved over the years, says Nelms. A few decades ago, communication with remote colleagues and customers took place over the phone. Then we added email, and now we use videoconferencing and online meeting tools. Nelms points out how communication is more continuous and real-time instead of being periodic.

Communication Example by Role

Consider the role of an engineering leader. She takes the vision for the company, which is expressed in terms of the business aspirations, and clarifies specifics for the engineering team. The high-level vision of "We want to become a leader in our industry" must be transformed into the engineering goal: "We will produce quality software solutions on time, meet customer needs, make the company highly successful, and become a leader in our industry." She must clarify the goal further by setting expectations in terms of standards, constraints, and acceptable targets. This communication needs to be delivered through town hall meetings of the engineering team. In these meetings, the team members take part actively, ask clarifying questions, and offer helpful suggestions to strengthen the goals further. Next, the goals need to be discussed with the small group of direct reports. They can then craft the execution plans. Finally, the engineering leader should make herself available to all team members with an open-door policy and encourage them to drop in for a discussion where she can engage in a one-on-one conversation.

Clarity in Communication

I cannot overemphasize the need for clarity in communication, which means knowing your audience and crafting your communication, especially for them. When I was leading software engineering, I learned what works when talking to those in management who are not technically savvy. I also knew it was essential to be highly technical and to-the-point in talking to the programmers on my team. Direct communication is all about being precise. However, you don't want to offend the person on the receiving end. It is important to avoid using highly specialized terminology only understood by practitioners when talking with laypeople. Expand any jargon in your writing for the first time. You can then use it in the rest of your communication.

Types of Leadership Communication

I categorize leadership communication by purpose, platform, and channel (Figure 7.1).

Purpose: It can be formal feedback, such as a performance review. Or an informal communication that a leader has when engaging with her team while walking around the office.

Platform: A large audience, as in a town hall meeting. Or a small group, usually, direct reports. Or one-on-one communication, where the leader interacts with just a follower.

Channels: The communication channels are of two types—verbal and nonverbal. We usually think about verbal communication. But the facial expression, body language, and

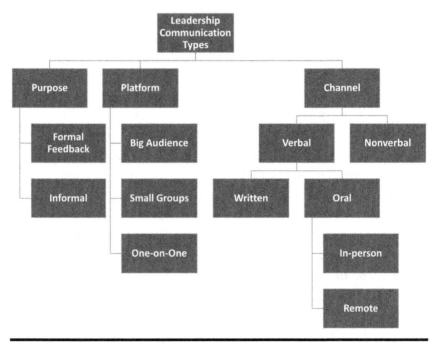

Figure 7.1   Types of communication.

eye contact are also important vehicles of communication. You can deliver verbal communication in a written medium, such as memo, email, and presentation slides. Today, you can also use multimedia channels on social networks. Oral communication can be in person or delivered remotely via audio and video recordings and streaming.

How to communicate in these different settings via different media is critical for leaders. We can enhance it with deliberate practice. Let us look at how to do it.

Purpose: Delivering Formal Feedback

A critical responsibility of a leader is team development. In executing this duty, they engage in a one-on-one feedback process. In recent years, there has been a lot of debate about how this feedback process should work. Most businesses have performance review cycles once or twice a year, and supervisors give feedback in written form, discussed, and recorded. I delivered many of these in my career. I can attest that there is always an element of discomfort involved in both giving and receiving feedback.

In the 2014 article, "Your Employees Want the Negative Feedback You Hate to Give,"[4] Zenger and Folkman shared some interesting statistics about feedback. These statistics were based on a survey that included 899 participants. Forty-nine percent of the respondents were from the United States. They concluded leaders are not comfortable giving constructive feedback. Over 90% of those who took part in the survey very much wanted to get feedback, even when negative. The key is to deliver the feedback in such a way to improve performance. The feedback process will be successful if you look at it with a mindset of developing the team member, and it goes much better when you show openness and invite participation (Figure 7.2).

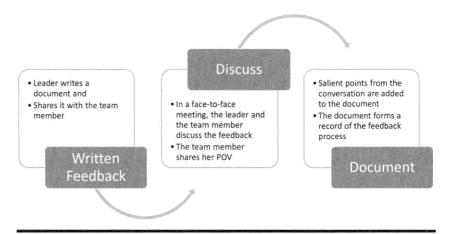

Figure 7.2   Formal feedback process.

Many leaders feel that giving corrective feedback is essential, but they are stingy with praise. Constructive feedback should call out the accomplishments and areas for improvement. Positive feedback tells your team members that you are interested in seeing them succeed and fosters their self-esteem. When you provide negative feedback, focus on the issues and not the person. Listening while giving feedback is very important. Nonverbal reactions can help you modulate your input to be more impactful.

Giving good feedback requires the leader to spend some time creating a strategy for delivering it. It should consider your past interactions and should include opportunities for improvement. It helps if you had not reserved the feedback for a once-a-year written review. Someone who received your praises throughout the year is more receptive to hearing your feedback on things she needs to improve.

Purpose: Informal Communication

Leaders have the opportunity for informal communication as much as they desire. These everyday communications are fruitful if the leaders make themselves approachable. Be humble. Ask, "What do you think?" Put your team members at ease. They will then be able to share their ideas, inputs, and feedback. A leader who enters an informal conversation to learn something always comes away from it, enriched in her knowledge. And learning happens when you listen.

Platform: Communication with a Big Audience

With a large audience, a considerable amount of effort should go into preparing the communication. The blog, "Guide for Presenting to Large Groups of People,"[5] has some good tips on preparing and delivering such speeches. Be sure to keep the communication focused on key takeaways from the message. If you are the only one speaking, you risk becoming boring. Engage the audience with questions, humor, and enthusiasm. When you do this remotely without video, vocal variety becomes extremely important. Think about the time when radio was the only medium available to inspire followers.

During the Quit India Movement, Mahatma Gandhi delivered such a speech. He had inspirational words but spoke them in a tone that sounded calm, collected, and impactful. In August 1942, millions of Indians listened to this speech. The speech was broadcast from Mumbai's Gowalia Tank and centered on a theme—do or die. Gandhi told Indians, "There is a mantra, short one, that I give you. You imprint it on your heart and let every breath of yours give an expression to it. The mantra is 'do or die.'"

Your speech to a large audience also needs a hook. Use a strategy and help the audience remember the purpose. You should repeat the theme several times and end the delivery with a summary of the goal.

Platform: Communication in Small Groups

Leaders conduct or attend many meetings with their teams throughout the day. Follow some basic guidelines in such small-group meetings. Conduct short meetings with well-defined agendas that keep the discussion focused on the purpose. Communicating to your team as a leader has one golden rule—don't hog the forum. The meetings in small groups are excellent opportunities to learn from your team members. You do that by listening.

Working with speakers of different languages can enhance your listening skills. Working with my Chinese team members who spoke Mandarin increased my ability to listen considerably. I was focusing all my efforts on comprehending what the speaker was saying. I wasn't trying to plan my response when they were talking.

Every member of a team has something worthwhile to contribute. Make it a point to draw out the introverts in your group to speak up. Create a two-way communication. Your success depends on it.

Platform: One-on-One Communication

When you engage in one-on-one conversations, listen more than you speak. When you listen, you put people at ease and make them willing partners in the conversation. Your action shows that you respect them. Make the person in the exchange comfortable with some small talk. When you express the desired team goal, be sure to emphasize what the team member's contribution means to that goal. A Knowledge@Wharton conversation,[6] quoted author, and educator Leah Weiss, who said only one in three people at work understand their role. One reason for this failure is inadequate or lousy communication. The smartphone presents a great temptation to multitask when you are engaged in an in-person conversation. Just don't do it. When you are in a critical face-to-face conversation, turn off your phone and focus entirely on the person you are talking with.

Channel: Verbal Communication

Written and oral are the two channels of verbal communication. Written communication is a critical skill that a leader must conquer. Today, distributed teams are the norm. Often, emails and instant messages are how communication happens. Express the right tone when you write, which is vital in both written and oral communication. When you are a leader, every word you write, whether in a memo or an email, influences the reader. Choose your words carefully. Be sure to include the aim of your communication. If you are looking for a response, be sure to say by when. If you want one of the team members to act, be sure you send it only to that person, unlike informational emails and memos. Readers respond better when the communication is short, simple, and concise rather than wordy. Emails are not appropriate under certain circumstances. It may be better to start a conversation when you are dealing with sensitive subjects. Praise is also better delivered in person.

Today, leaders can use various tools on the internet to communicate. You can write a blog or short posts on Twitter or Instagram. No matter what medium you use, keep the content professional and factual. The responsibility of the leader is to ensure that the communication is unbiased and serves specific goals.

Oral communication can happen in person or through remote channels. Earlier, we discussed the formal and informal communication that occurs in the one-on-one channel, in person. Email and phone are now the de facto channels for leaders to engage with their teams. The coronavirus pandemic made this even more critical. Given this, you need to make sure you are as effective on the phone, email, and tools such as Zoom and WebEx as you are in person. You can't see the other person on the phone, and you are limited to verbal responses. Video communication removes this limitation. But often we may experience technical issues because of poor network connectivity. Be sure not to multitask when you are on a remote call. There is nothing more demoralizing for your team member than to find out that you were writing an email while engaging in the conversation.

Channel: Nonverbal Communication

Your body communicates more than you can tell.

Your authenticity comes through the nonverbal signals you send out. If your listener hears you say one thing but sees a contradiction in your body language, she could very well decide you are dishonest. Your nonverbal signals may also convey a message that you don't care. In the same way, the emotions and facial expressions invoked by hearing what you say can tell you much more about how your listener received it than a verbal response. Your ability as a leader to read these nonverbal signals, such as facial expressions, gestures, posture, and tone of voice, can be tremendously helpful in modulating your communication, which comes from practice. Pay full attention to the person you are talking with to understand the body language. Even in a small group or large audience, you can tell a lot more by a nonverbal response such as bored looks, slouching, and multitasking, so pay attention to them. You will get better with time.

Master the Art of Communication

Your success as a leader depends on how well you communicate. Understand the communication types and use them appropriately, depending on the purpose, platform, and channel. Learn the nuances associated with each type of communication, practice, and become better at it. And keep improving your listening skills.

Practice

- Next time you are in a conversation, focus on what your partner is saying and listen actively. Hold your silence and repeat what you heard mentally before responding.
- Join Toastmasters or a speech club to practice your verbal communication.
- Start a blog to write your thoughts on what matters to you.

Communication—Questions to Ask Yourself

- Am I an active listener?
- Am I open to the views of others and reflect on them?
- Do I craft my communication based on the audience?

Notes

1. David Novak, "Follow Indra Nooyi's Example: Become a Leader People Are Excited to Follow," *CNBC.com*, September 12, 2018, accessed June 9, 2021, https://www.cnbc.com/2018/09/12/pepsico-indra-nooyi-be-a-leader-people-want-to-follow.html.
2. Chris Riback, "John Chambers, Connecting the Dots," *Working Capital Review*, October 17, 2018, accessed June 9, 2021, https://workingcapitalreview.com/2018/10/john-chambers-connecting-the-dots/.
3. Jacob Morgan, "The Best Leaders Are Great Communicators Says Former Discover Financial CEO David Nelms," *The Future of Work*, May 26, 2020, accessed June 9, 2021, https://medium.com/jacob-morgan/the-best-leaders-are-great-communicators-says-former-discover-financial-ceo-david-nelms-fe08aa826d04.

4. Jack Zenger & Joseph Folkman, "Your Employees Want the Negative Feedback You Hate to Give," *Harvard Business Review*, January 15, 2014, accessed June 9, 2021, from https://hbr.org/2014/01/your-employees-want-the-negative-feedback-you-hate-to-give.

5. Dom Barnard, "Guide for Presenting to Large Groups of People," *Virtual Speech*, November 14, 2017, accessed June 9, 2021, https://virtualspeech.com/blog/guide-for-presenting-to-large-groups-of-people.

6. Interview with Leah Weiss, "Does Your Company Need a VP of Kindness?" *Knowledge@Wharton*, May 23, 2018, accessed June 9, 2021, from https://knowledge.wharton.upenn.edu/article/why-kindness-matters-in-modern-work/.

Resources

Dale Carnegie, *How to Win Friends and Influence People* (Simon and Schuster, 1998).

Kerry Patterson et al., *Crucial Conversations: Tools for Talking When Stakes Are High* (McGraw-Hill Education, 2011).

Chapter 8

We Can Work It Out

"We Can Work It Out" is my anthem for when I encounter difficult situations and conflicts. This title kindled my thoughts about writing this book on leadership. Leaders who possess a superior ability to negotiate can take their organizations to outstanding success. These leaders do their research, understand the consequences of different strategies, and work with the other party for an outcome that is a win-win for all involved. Leaders who understand the negotiation process and tap into their emotional intelligence can work it out in difficult circumstances.

About the Song

The Beatles recorded this song during the *Rubber Soul* album sessions. It was first issued as a double A-side single with "Day Tripper" in December 1965. The song is another excellent juxtaposition of the

DOI: 10.4324/9781003267546-10

songwriters' mental states. Paul is very optimistic in his lyrics, while John's middle eight comes across as being impatient with the situation—let's get on with it, life is too short. The Beatles were masters at this, with John usually taking the pessimistic stand to Paul's upbeat lyrics.

We Can Work It Out—Negotiating and Managing Conflict

If there is desire for change, it must be a subject for negotiation, and if there is negotiation, it must be rooted in mutual respect and concern for the rights of others.

—John F. Kennedy[1]

Paul McCartney initially wrote "We Can Work It Out" about his relationship with girlfriend Jane.[2] He acknowledged that the lyrics might have been personal. They possibly helped him work out his thoughts, say the things he wanted to say, and save a trip to the psychiatrist. This song lifts my spirits and helps me face situations of conflict. I believe we can work it out.

You can resolve personal conflicts in multiple ways. One of them is to walk away from the situation. Teenagers are good at walking away when their parents try to address a difficult problem, but we are aware we cannot always do that. You may postpone discussing the conflict, but it can fester unless you do that for the right reason; for example, think through the situation with a definite time to resolution. Often, you can persuade those who disagree with you. But this may cause the other party to develop resentment toward you if not handled properly. The postponement and persuasion strategies are typical reasons marriages fall apart.

Leaders do not have the luxury of ignoring or postponing conflicts. If they do, the consequences can be pretty disastrous.

In "The Leader's Role in Managing Conflicts,"[3] Guttman describes what happened at a billion-dollar financial services firm. The firm's CEO came up through the ranks and possessed a friendly leadership style. Two executives on his team experienced a conflict. He tried to manage the disagreement by having a separate meeting with each of them. For a while, it seemed the problem had disappeared. However, the conflict lingered and became so big that a third party needed to be brought in to resolve it. Guttman says leaders cannot expect to be a "nice guy" in conflict management, and they also cannot be a "tough guy," where teams would not be comfortable bringing up conflicts when they exist. Learning to manage the tension between these two extremes is a critical leadership skill to develop. Guttman tells the story of Roy Anise, senior vice president of planning and information at Philip Morris USA, who discovered how much of a "tough guy" he was and corrected his behavior with the help of a coach to become better.

In my experience as a leader, the best way to resolve conflicts is to negotiate.

Conflict Resolution Is a Key Leadership Skill

I spent several years building a company with my cofounders, and my responsibility was to lead engineering teams. Conflicts are an everyday occurrence in an entrepreneur's life. The founders cannot agree on a strategy for expansion. A customer wants a bugfix in a day, and the engineering team needs two. A marketing manager wants an additional feature in two weeks, but the product manager says the effort will take a month. Sales blame the product as the reason for not being able to sell. Team members clash with each other on which tool to use in development. A candidate with great potential likes the position but asks for a salary that is too high. I experienced them all. There are many situations when a leader has to resolve conflicts within the team and across teams, negotiate with vendors, and take care of customers. The approach to doing each of these varies, depending on the context.

Conflicts are not harmful. In fact, the tension created by conflicts is actually good because you get to experience multiple perspectives. But when the disagreement leads to undesired outcomes, that is bad. Not just for those involved in the conflict, but for those around. A discord between two teammates is a typical occurrence in the work environment. When this happens, the entire team suffers. As a team leader, you need to resolve the conflict as quickly as possible before it escalates into a full-blown demoralizing situation. The conflict between cofounders could cause the death of a start-up. Disputes between business partners, if unresolved, may lead to a poor reputation, and third parties may hesitate to deal with you when you need it. Conflicts with customers are deadly. Avoid them at all costs, but when you can't, handle the situation with care.

One Orange, Two Chefs

A leader must remain calm when faced with a conflict.

A commercial kitchen is one place that is teeming with conflicts. Besides the intense heat created by all the stoves and ovens, the personalities of those who work in such kitchens produce many dramatic moments. In one such kitchen, two sous-chefs got into a conflict. They both needed an orange for each of their recipes, but only one orange was available. Both of them claimed the orange was theirs. The autocratic executive chef (think Gordon Ramsay) had enough of their arguments. He grabbed a cleaver close at hand, brought it down on the orange, and offered one-half to each sous-chef. One chef was making a sauce with orange juice for his scallop dish, and the other chef was baking a cake that needed candied orange peel for garnishing. By cutting the orange in half, there was not enough ingredient for either chef to create their perfect dishes. They settled for something they were not happy with.

The executive chef tasted the sauce. He didn't like it. He glanced at the garnish and it was not up to his standard. If only he, as the leader, had taken a few minutes to find out the actual need of each chef, he could have helped them with the suggestion that resulted in a much better outcome. By peeling the orange, the rind could go to the chef who was making the cake and the juice to the chef making the sauce. Leadership during conflicts requires cool heads.

Diane Musho Hamilton, an award-winning professional mediator, author, facilitator, and teacher of Zen meditation, says,[4] that if we want to resolve conflicts, we need to start from a place where we don't think the other party is wrong. She advocates using sitting meditation to achieve inner peace as the first step in conflict resolution.

When you start with the thinking "You are wrong," you are already creating an obstacle in resolving conflicts. Think of disagreement as not the issue. How you react to it is the problem. Once you understand this, you can deal with any dispute efficiently.

Do Not Negotiate from Positions

Negotiation experts Roger Fisher and William Ury[5] make an interesting argument for not taking positions in negotiating. They say that taking stances in negotiations results in less-than-acceptable outcomes, inefficient processes, and damaged relationships. Instead, they propose an alternative called "principled negotiation or negotiation on the merits." Instead of seeing the persons involved as friends or adversaries, look at them as problem-solvers. The goals of the problem-solvers are to resolve the problem efficiently, maintain goodwill, and treat people involved with care. Irrespective of whether you trust the other party, proceed with the negotiation. Consider the interests of all involved.

Explore multiple options and establish a criterion for evaluating the possibilities.

One of my star performers in the engineering team wanted transfer to another department. The transfer could be denied by me easily. But I did not take an adversarial position. Instead, I congratulated him and negotiated a delay of one week in his transfer. During that one week, I asked him to train another team member on his existing responsibilities. The criterion I established for this situation was the long-term reputation for my leadership, one that valued the interest of the individual's goals above the difficulties I would face in replacing him with an equally excellent performer.

Steps in Resolving Conflicts

The first step in resolving a conflict is to agree about its existence. Sometimes we are afraid to handle a conflict and sweep it under the rug. That can fester and blow up. The next step is to understand the root cause of the discord. For example, in a team conflict, perhaps we did not define the team members' roles clearly. Maybe the communication between the leader and the team members is not good. Conceivably the team members are not communicating well with each other. In a conflict, make sure you hear the perspectives of all the parties involved. Listening is a critical skill to employ in conflict management, and so is communication.

Negotiating Is a Key Leadership Skill

The key to resolving conflicts is learning to be an excellent negotiator. Negotiation skills have their start in your childhood, wanting to stay up late, having one more scoop of ice cream, sleeping over at a friend's house—the list goes on. We see students haggle with their teachers about their grades. Negotiations are at work with salary raises, promotions, and perks. We engage when we disagree with the other party on a decision.

As a leader, your negotiation skills determine how well your company can succeed in a competitive world. Can you work it out with your partners? Are you able to have coopetition instead of competition? Will you be able to negotiate a good deal with a customer? Can you collaborate with your vendors on a contract that maximizes benefits for both of you? Do your actions inspire your team to go above and beyond by working with their intrinsic motivation?

Negotiation Process

The negotiation process begins with research to understand the facts (Figure 8.1). If you don't have all the details in hand,

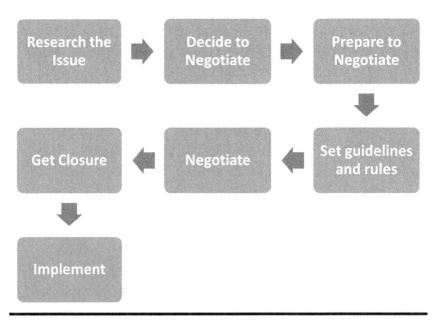

Figure 8.1   Negotiation process.

you will be at a disadvantage when you walk into the negotiation meeting. You do not want to be blindsided by something that the other party brings up during the process. Get help from your team in collecting the facts. Then analyze them not only from your point of view but also from the other party's perspective.

A Handy Tool to Help with Negotiations

In all negotiations, you should know what to do if there is no agreement between the parties. A tool called "Best Alternative to a Negotiated Agreement (BATNA)"[6] is handy to have. My friend says, "BATNA is like the Swiss army. The value is in its potential, but having a good one ready to go greatly reduces the chances you'll need it." BATNA requires a robust analysis process. During this process, you may discover a lot of valuable facts to manage the negotiation. It is essential to understand your BATNA and also the BATNA of the other party.

Fisher and Ury call out the following important steps to understand your BATNA:

1. Understand all the different actions you can take if the negotiation fails.
2. Consider each of the alternatives and evaluate the likely outcome and its desirability.
3. Choose the one that gives you the most desirable alternative.
4. Determine the least desirable alternative you would accept.
5. If the desirability of the agreement proposed to you is lower than your least desirable alternative, choose your best alternative. If the agreement proposed is more desirable than the least desirable alternative, accept the agreement.

Here is a very simplified example of BATNA from my experience of buying a software development tool for my team. After doing extensive research, we chose two vendors whose products we deemed quite comparable. The initial budget for the product was $11,000 per year. *Vendor A* offered the tool for $11,500, a price she could not negotiate any further. So my BATNA is $11,500. *Vendor B*'s initial offer was at $12,500. Between them, *Vendor B* had a better client base, better financials, and excellent customer support. During the negotiations, I informed *Vendor B* I was getting a much better price from *Vendor A*. I also knew that because of quarter-end, *Vendor B* was keen on making the sale. I would have to pay at least $11,500 irrespective of which vendor I went with. *Vendor B* knew my alternative and agreed to the price of $11,500.

However, I didn't settle for BATNA. I aimed for my initial budget. By offering to serve as a reference customer for the tool, I brought down the price of *Vendor B* to my initial plan of $10,000. You should know your BATNA, but always keep your goal in mind. Your BATNA may change midway through negotiations because of some events unknown at the start. Not all factors that go into using BATNA are quantifiable. BATNA is a tool. Just like with other tools, how you use it is entirely up to you.

It is good to play out the scenarios of how the negotiation might go. Then, when you walk into a negotiation meeting, you will come across as confident. Note that being confident differs from coming across as arrogant. You will want to keep in mind that your tone, how you carry yourself, and how you address the other party are all critical in conveying your position. Be mindful of the cultural differences. If you are going to negotiate with someone from a different culture, learn about what works in that culture.

Getting Better at Negotiating

Some are inherently better at negotiating than others. Above all, they are great at people skills. Emotional intelligence is fundamental to building this skill. While some are born with it, everyone can learn it. *Daniel Goleman*'s 1995 book coined and made popular the term "Emotional Intelligence."[7] Since then, the concept has seen many advances. If you are not familiar with it, I urge you to read the book. The fundamental competencies of emotional intelligence, such as self-awareness, self-regulation, self-motivation, empathy, and effective relationships, all come into play in negotiating successfully.

In the world of education, good learning programs start with the mentality of "start from where they're at," which is also true for negotiations. To understand where they are at, listen to those you are negotiating with. Empathy, one of the basic competencies of emotional intelligence, is essential to good listening. Put yourself in other people's shoes and recognize their emotions.

When you express your thoughts with empathy, the other person will respond in kind. The entire process of negotiation will be less antagonizing.

As the head of software engineering, I helped my team negotiate release dates, features, and customer support. These negotiations involved several stakeholders with different interests. Release dates were critical for the sales and marketing functions since they involve promises made to the customers. The software developers held themselves to a high standard of quality software. We understood the trade-offs between release date and features and good enough and perfect quality software. The team comprehended release dates were important and empathized with sales to find a mutually agreeable date, feature-set, and acceptable quality metrics.

Similarly, negotiating how quickly we can resolve a support issue requires understanding the customer's pain. For example, a software bug is preventing a customer from performing a business function. You listen and understand what workarounds are possible to contain the customer's pain. If no workaround is possible, you need to explore other options. After negotiating with a team member who agrees to work over the weekend, you promise the customer your team will find a fix in two days. Your negotiation with the team member should acknowledge that she is giving up her personal time to do this and compensate for it.

When you are in negotiations that you perceive to be difficult, don't skirt the issues. It is best to discuss and lay them out in the open. Imagine yourself in the other person's situation to see their points of view.

We Can Work It Out

In "We're All Innocently Out of Touch,"[8] Morgan Housel, the author of the book *The Psychology of Money*, talks about how we are all so removed from everyone else's thinking. We all have good intentions and want to do the right thing. But each of us is unique. Your experiences are unique to you. You are out of touch with where the other person is coming from. Even though Housel's discussion is on investing, you can learn from what he says about starting with the assumption that we don't know where the other person is coming from. When you remember this, you will think through the points of view of those you are negotiating with. You are less likely to fit things into your frame of reference built on your experience. You will understand and empathize with the other person, which is key to better negotiation and finding a mutually beneficial outcome.

Practice

■ Next time you are getting ready for a negotiation, such as a partnership with a third-party vendor, go through the process of BATNA. Discuss the details with your team.

Negotiating—Questions to Ask Yourself

■ How good am I in seeking to resolve conflicts?
■ Do I consciously explore a winning strategy for all involved in the negotiation?
■ Am I good at bringing all views to bear on the negotiations?

Notes

1. John F. Kennedy, Address before the General Assembly of the United Nations, September 25, 1961.
2. "We Can Work It Out," *Beatles Music History: The In-Depth Story behind the Songs of The Beatles*, accessed June 7, 2021, http://www.beatlesebooks.com/we-can-work-it-out.
3. Howard M. Guttman, "The Leader's Role in Managing Conflict," *Leader to Leader*, December 9, 2003, accessed June 11, 2021, https://doi.org/10.1002/ltl.63.
4. Diane Musho Hamilton, *Everything Is Workable: A Zen Approach to Conflict Resolution* (Shambhala, 2013).
5. William Ury & Roger Fisher, *Getting to Yes: Negotiating Agreement without Giving in* (Penguin Books, 2011).
6. Ibid.
7. Daniel Goleman, *Emotional Intelligence: Why It Can Matter More than IQ* (Random House Publishing Group, September 27, 2005).
8. Morgan Housel, "We're All Innocently Out of Touch," *Collaborative Fund*, November 17, 2017, accessed June 11, 2021, https://www.collaborativefund.com/blog/were-all-out-of -touch/.

Resources

Diane Musho Hamilton, *Everything Is Workable: A Zen Approach to Conflict Resolution* (Shambhala, 2013).

Program on Negotiation—Executive Education, Harvard Law School, accessed June 11, 2021, https://www.pon.harvard.edu/executive -education/.

Roger Fisher et al., *Getting to Yes: Negotiating Agreement without Giving In* (Penguin Books, 2011).

Chapter 9

Any Time at All

"Any Time at All" reminds me I must be available to those I lead and be approachable. We have many demands on our time and attention. Leaders who make time for their teams increase the opportunities to communicate their vision and hear feedback. When you practice approachability as a leader, you signal to your team that you are available, open to conversations, and seeking to collaborate. Leaders who make time for their families, friends, and loved ones live a more satisfying life. Leaders who make time available for themselves take care of their needs and health. They have the energy and spirit to carry on with all the demands. This chapter talks about how to do that.

About the Song

The Beatles recorded "Any Time at All" in 1964 and released it the same year. John was its primary

DOI: 10.4324/9781003267546-11   **123**

composer. The song features in *A Hard Day's Night* album. *The Beatles Music History*[1] goes into great detail about the recording. It says:

While both John and Paul proclaim that it was fully written by Lennon, the evidence may suggest otherwise. This can be said because of the circumstances regarding the recording session for the song. While in the studio, they recorded seven takes but were then convinced that it needed something more. They proceeded with recording other songs and, during a 90-minute break, came up with an instrumental section for the song. This section is highlighted by an intricate passage on piano which is played by Paul. This may very well indicate that McCartney had at least a slight hand in the composition.

Any Time at All—Availability

Caring leaders are generous with their time and attention.

A paradox of the modern world is productivity. We create more and more innovations to save time. However, we don't have enough time to do everything that we want to do. Time is precious. There are so many things that compete for our attention. Today, smartphones tether us to the internet, and it is easy to be physically present but not be accessible. It is common for executives to be on their phones checking their texts and phone messages while attending a meeting. We see parents glued to their phones while monitoring what is going on with their children's sports games.

Demands on Your Time and Attention

Several relationships compete for a leader's time and attention. Leaders have to be accessible to their team members, colleagues, partners, and customers. They also must make sure they are available to their family and friends. Society also looks to leaders in times of need. Leaders must also pay attention to their own well-being. It is like the oxygen mask used in an airplane. In a crisis, you need to use an oxygen mask on yourself first before you can help your children. A leader needs to take care of herself first so that she can lead effectively (Figure 9.1).

When you are leading a team, being accessible is key to the team's success. The team members expect the leader to provide them with direction. They rely on their leader for coaching when they encounter a roadblock. They like a sounding board when faced with critical decision-making.

Figure 9.1 Relationships.

When you are part of a large organization, spend time with your colleagues in other teams. You can understand the organization's overall goals when you talk to them and become strategic in your leadership. Organizational partners deserve your attention and time so that you can collaborate and help each other. When your team is customer-facing, focus on customers and pay immediate attention to their needs.

Accessibility starts with approachability. Most of the organizations are hierarchical. As you grow in your career, there will be a few layers between you and the front line. Irrespective of where they are in the hierarchy, be approachable to everyone in the organization, which is critical to your success as a leader.

Above all, you must be available to your family. Your son may need guidance on how to approach the upcoming exam. There is a game coming up where your daughter needs coaching. Your wife hopes you will be at an event where she is receiving an award.

Are you available to yourself? People who don't have time to take care of themselves compromise their health. Insomnia is a common symptom of poor health. Christopher Barnes, Professor of Organizational Behavior at the University of Washington's Foster School of Business, has done several studies[2] about the effect of not having sufficient sleep on the behavior of individuals. The findings show poor sleep habits lead to poor judgment and affect creativity. His research shows that leaders who do not get enough sleep are bad at leading their teams. They mistreat employees and create a toxic working environment.

A note on availability—don't expect to be available to everyone, all the time, at the same priority, at every point in your life. Adjust your preferences and strategies depending on where you are in your life, which I talk about in Chapter 16, "When I'm Sixty-Four."

Make Yourself Approachable

The first step to increasing your accessibility is to become approachable. There are several strategies you can use to develop your approachability.

Communication with your team members is critical to show you are approachable. Show this by making small talk, greetings, and smiles, and share your failings with the team. Talk about specific failures and what they taught you.

Daniel Haughton retired as the Chair of Lockheed in 1976. He was a leader who did not hesitate to talk about his mistakes. In "The Failure-Tolerant Leader,"[3] the authors recount a story about Dan, when he was the CEO, and a mistake he shared with his team. When Douglas Aircraft was struggling, its founder Howard Hughes called Dan and asked him to buy the company. The founder of McDonnell Aircraft Corporation, Jimmy McDonnell, was also interested in buying it. Dan said not listening to Howard was one of the biggest mistakes he made. He accepted that if he had bought Douglas Aircraft, he could have avoided costly moves by consolidating Lockheed's operations in Southern California.

Approachability, Attitude, and Authenticity

Have you heard about the power of four words, "What do you think?" Bill Marriott, the founder of the Marriott Hotel chain, tells a story about the US President David Eisenhower on his blog *Marriott on the Move.*[4]

In 1954, Bill was a student at the US Navy Supply Corps School. He went home for the Christmas holidays. His family had a farm in Virginia. Through his connections with the US Secretary of Agriculture, his father invited the then President of the United States, Eisenhower, to visit them. His staff had set up quail and pheasants for shooting since Eisenhower loved the sports. The weather was cold, and 10 degrees below freezing. The staff wanted to find out if the President would still like to go out in the cold to shoot the birds or stay indoors by the fire. Bill was standing behind the President. Eisenhower turned to him and asked, "What do you think, Bill?" Though a little flustered, Bill answered it was freezing, and staying by the fire seemed like a good idea. Eisenhower agreed, and they stayed inside. Bill says the four words "What do you think?" make you feel free to express your opinions. You hope that what you say matters and it will produce results. They make a leader approachable.

In a *Rolling Stone* interview, Pete Townshend of the "Who" described the difference between John Lennon and Paul McCartney.[5] When he met Paul, Townshend was thoroughly impressed by how easy it was to converse with him. Paul seemed to like him genuinely for who he was, making him an even bigger fan of Paul. Authenticity makes you more approachable.

Vulnerability Enhances Approachability

Another way to become approachable is to ask for help[6] when your decisions can use some input from your team. When you acknowledge you don't possess the answers to all the questions and invite help, that signals you are an open-minded individual. It tells your team you value their opinions and expertise. Your team members then would not hesitate to ask for your opinions, help, and guidance. A vulnerable leader sends a message that she is not someone on a pedestal and is genuinely approachable.

Informal Engagement

One of the best ways to become approachable is to practice "Management by Wandering (or Walking) Around (MBWA)." The management thought leader and author, Tom Peters, discovered the term during his visit to Hewlett Packard in 1979.

While researching for the book "In Search of Excellence,"[7] Tom and his coauthor Bob Waterman visited Hewlett Packard (HP) in Palo Alto, California. In his 2021 book, *Excellence Now: Extreme Humanism*, Tom recalls meeting the president of HP, John Young. He heard about the "HP Way" and its cornerstone, "management by wandering around," during that visit. When walking around the office, you create informal opportunities to talk to the team instead of formal meetings. You listen to what your colleagues say, and learn from it. The ability to speak to a leader openly about any topic makes the leader approachable in the team members' eyes, irrespective of where they are in the organization.

While wandering, there are many opportunities to ask questions. There are multiple benefits in inviting questions from your team members, colleagues, partners, and others. First, it shows you value their opinion; second, the invitation boosts their self-esteem; third, the team sees you are approachable. Inputs from diverse stakeholders bring multiple ideas in addressing a problem you are trying to solve and help you see different perspectives. Often, team members hesitate to give their input to their leaders. Once you become approachable, they would voice their thoughts freely. Note that it is not enough to engage with active listening. There has to be some follow-through that shows that you actually listened.

In your calendar, reserve some time for being available to those who might need you. Many organizations promote an "open-door" policy, encouraging everyone to talk to the top leaders irrespective of hierarchy. Even if your organization doesn't have a formal policy, nothing prevents you from practicing it.

Remote Teams

Another way to signal you are accessible is through emails and instant messages. When the pandemic struck, many of us had to adopt a work from home policy. We lost the opportunity for physical communication. However, we can practice informal communication even if our physical presence is not possible. My experience with remote work began in the 1980s when I worked from home before and after my child was born. I experienced firsthand being at home, working by myself, away from the rest of my fellow team members. Later, I had the opportunity and responsibility to lead distributed teams spread across the world. I had informal communication by emailing a remote team member or picking up the phone and calling them about their well-being. I visited them once a quarter and had many one-to-one sessions, and talked to them during team lunches and dinners while I was there. Today, there are so many tools available for remote communication. There are messaging tools such as Slack, video conference tools such as Zoom, and the ever-useful phone.

When your team members and others realize you are accessible, they get the confidence to reach out to you for any help they need. Some of them may want to use you as a sounding board. Some may look to you to be a mentor or coach. Others may wish for just a sympathetic listener.

It Is Not Rocket Science

What do I mean by being available? It may be as simple as answering emails promptly. When the team is expecting a response, there is nothing worse than delaying the answer. Even if you don't know the answer, tell them you received the email, and you will respond shortly. When you are part of a meeting, always be on time. Even better, be there a little early to engage in small talk and establish rapport with those attending the discussion. Punctuality sends a message that you value the time contributed by others. If you are late, don't forget to apologize. Many of us pride ourselves on punctuality, but we all have been late occasionally. But don't be a chronic latecomer.

As a leader, activities fill your days. Sometimes you may go from one meeting to another, which is not conducive to being accessible, so set boundaries. If you cannot devote your time and attention fully, it is OK to say, not now, and set up another time to talk.

Of course, there are only so many hours in a day, and you cannot be available to everyone all the time. Therefore, prioritizing your tasks is important. It is a juggling act. You will get better as you practice it. A technique used in project management called "Time Boxing"[8] can be helpful in managing your time. But you can extend it to manage your personal time as well.

Customers Need You

We talked about being there for to members of your organization. Customers deserve the same treatment. When a leader is available to the customers, their satisfaction goes way up. Don't wait for a crisis to be in touch with customers. Of course, there may not be enough time to talk to every customer. You can scale the attention to your customers by being available to your team. If you are present for your team, they will then be inspired to be attentive to customers. The multiplication effort makes it scalable.

Some leaders are extraordinary in making themselves available to their customers. A CNN article[9] on Steve Jobs called him an outlier and talked about how Steve interacted with customers above and beyond what a CEO would do regarding customer service, paying a lot of attention, and exercising patience. Scott Steckley, an Apple customer, emailed Jobs he had been waiting an incredibly long time for a computer repair. Little did he expect Jobs to pick up the phone and call him. On the phone, Jobs introduced himself and apologized for the delay. He said the delay was not really anybody's fault, "just one of those things." Steckley calmed down, saying he understood. Behaviors such as exhibited by Steve Jobs endeared him to his customers. He was accessible to customers.

Family and Friends

Your family and friends need you as much as your work. Set aside time for your family. If you set boundaries at work, you will have time to spend with your family. You can inform people at work that you will not be available to them after certain hours. For many of us, flexible working hours help us be available to our family when needed. In the early days of my start-up, I used to send emails late at night after spending time with my family in the evening. I didn't realize how these emails would appear to my team members until one of my senior members asked me not to do so because it seemed urgent to be receiving emails so late in the day. In retrospect, I should have sent those emails with delayed delivery, which would have satisfied my team members, and accommodated my need to work at night and be available to my family in the evening.

Taking Time for Yourself

Many leaders resist caring for themselves. You can't be there for others unless you are in excellent form. Leadership is challenging. But it doesn't have to be stressful. Take care of yourself physically and mentally. Physical self-care involves eating right, getting adequate sleep, and exercising. Mental self-care consists in finding activities to stimulate your mind, avoiding activities that are harmful to your mind, and having good relationships with your family, friends, and colleagues.[10]

Make Availability a Leadership Priority

Approachability and accessibility are keys to making yourself available to your team, colleagues, family, and friends. Leaders who make themselves available reap the benefits of highly motivated teams and better relationships all around. Don't forget to be there for yourself. Use productivity tools to manage your time. Use every opportunity you get to talk to your teams. Make communication a priority.

Practice

- Start practicing informal communication consciously. Keep a journal and document what happened over 100 days. Do you see any changes in your work relationships?

Availability—Questions to Ask Yourself

- What can I do to make myself more accessible?
- What would my team members say about my availability?
- Do I take care of myself?

Notes

1. "Any Time at All," *The Beatles Music History*, accessed August 2, 2021, http://www.beatlesebooks.com/any-time-at-all.
2. Christopher M. Barnes, "Sleep Well, Lead Better," *Harvard Business Review*, 2018, accessed June 11, 2021, https://hbr.org /2018/09/sleep-well-lead-better.
3. Richard Farson & Ralph Keyes, "The Failure-Tolerant Leader," *Harvard Business Review*, 2002, accessed June 11, 2021, https:// hbr.org/2002/08/the-failure-tolerant-leader.
4. Bill Marriott, "What Do You Think," *Marriott on the Move*, February 19, 2014, accessed June 11, 2021, https://www.blogs .marriott.com/marriott-on-the-move/2014/02/what-do-you-think .html.

5. Jann S. Wenner, "Pete Townshend: The Rolling Stone Interview, Part Two," *Rolling Stone*, September 28, 1968, accessed June 11, 2021, https://www.rollingstone.com/music/music-news/pete-townshend-the-rolling-stone-interview-part-two-38602/.
6. See Chapter 5, Help!
7. Tom Peters & Robert H. Waterman Jr., *In Search of Excellence, Lessons from America's Best-Run Companies* (Harper Collins, 2004).
8. Matthias Orgler, "7 Secrets to Master Timeboxing," *Dreimannzelt Adventures*, April 21, 2016, accessed June 11, 2021, https://medium.com/dreimannzelt-adventures/7-secrets-to-master-timeboxing-66a744ea9175.
9. Mark Milian, "Steve Jobs Fielded Some Customer Service Requests," *CNN*, November 23, 2011, accessed June 11, 2021, https://www.cnn.com/2011/11/22/tech/innovation/jobs-excerpt-customer-service/index.html.
10. See more on this in Chapter 16, "When I'm Sixty-Four."

Resources

Dale Carnegie, *How To Win Friends and Influence People* (Simon and Schuster, 1998).
Daniel H. Pink, *Drive: The Surprising Truth About What Motivates Us* (Riverhead Books, 2011).
Tom J. Peters & Robert H. Waterman Jr., *In Search of Excellence, Lessons from America's Best-Run Companies.* (Harper Business, 2006).

Chapter 10

I Me Mine

"I Me Mine" are the words of those who always put themselves ahead of others. These words remind me not to hoard all the power and decision-making as a leader. Leaders empower their teams by sharing responsibilities, providing growth opportunities, and fostering a collaborative environment. It starts with delegating and building trust. Empowerment depends on the team member's skills. The leader has the responsibility to involve team members in activities and training that develop their capabilities. This chapter discusses strategies to build empowered teams. Outstanding leaders create more leaders.

About the Song

George Harrison wrote the song "I Me Mine," released in May 1970. The song was one of two compositions on the *Let It Be* album and about the eternal

DOI: 10.4324/9781003267546-12

problem of ego. He liked the title enough to call his autobiography the same in 1980. When I listen to George chanting these words in the song, I am reminded of what not to do as a leader.

I Me Mine—Empowering

No man will make a great business who wants to do it all himself or to get all the credit for doing it.

—Andrew Carnegie[1]

Jeff Bezos, Amazon's founder and executive chair, talks about Type 1 and Type 2 decisions in his 1997 letter to the shareholders.[2] Type 1 decisions are those with consequences and are irreversible or almost irreversible. Once you make such a decision, you cannot retract. You cannot backtrack if you don't like the outcome. He calls them one-way doors, and you must make these decisions with tremendous care. They require methodical deliberation and thought. The other type of decision is the Type 2 decision and most decisions are of this type. Bezos calls them two-way doors. You can reverse the decision—reopen the door and go back. Small groups or individuals with high judgment can make these decisions. By delegating Type 2 decisions, you will empower the teams to increase inventions, he says. Empowerment is the key to building capable organizations, such as Amazon.

Empowering Your Team Is a Critical Leadership Skill

If you hoard the power of decision-making, you cannot grow as a leader. It stifles creativity and growth and limits what your team can achieve. In such an environment, you tend to lose your self-esteem and spirit. We see a lot of attrition under such a leader. Leaders who consciously learn to delegate and empower their team members bring out the best in them. They grow their teams and create a thriving work environment.

Toni Morrison was an American novelist and a professor. In discussing the greater good,[3] Morrison talks about her students who are graduating and getting a job. She says she tells them that those with freedom need to pay it forward by freeing someone else. If you possess power, empower someone else.

One of the most important leadership responsibilities is to establish your successor. I used to ask myself this question: "What will happen if I get hit by a bus?" It sounds a little macabre. But leaders should be prepared for such eventualities. You cannot hope to deliver on this responsibility if you don't empower your team. You need to be deliberate and methodical in your delegation and empowerment when you want to create a successor.

In Retail Solutions, the company I cofounded, the cofounders took care of the start-up's needs. We divided the responsibilities among the four of us. Product development was mine, and I delivered retail analytics to our early customers, such as Procter & Gamble, PepsiCo, and Unilever. I worked with a graphic company to design our logo, even though this was not a product development job. As we grew, we brought in more people to do the various activities. We empowered these new employees and made it possible for us to scale. Over time, I coached and grew my successor. When I retired, my successor stepped in and took over without missing a beat. For a start-up to succeed, scaling is crucial. You can do that only by growing an organization that is empowered.

An Empowered Organization

W.L. Gore & Associates, Inc.,[4] founded by Bill and Vieve Gore in 1958, is a prime example of how empowerment works. Their employees are all called "associates." They are part owners of the company through the associate stock ownership plan. The company is private and prefers to stay that way. Public companies often take the short-term view. But Gore's culture is about taking a long-term view when making business decisions, and staying private helps them do that. Gore has over 3400 unique inventions worldwide. These are in fields such as electronics, medical devices, and polymer processing. Gore's 11,000 employees work in offices in over 25 countries, and the company earns $3.8 billion in annual revenues.

Gore's website articulates their culture[5]:

We're more than employees; we're trusted stewards of our business. Each of us makes commitments that help drive the business, and we work together in our lattice communications structure. In this structure, we collaborate and build connections without the constraints of traditional chains of command — giving us the freedom to encourage and support each other's growth and development. It's an environment in which highly motivated people thrive and where we are able to bring our unique talents and diverse perspectives to problem-solve and collectively get our work done.

How does empowerment work at Gore? Here is an example:

One of the Gore manufacturing teams felt an outsourced job was slowing them down by creating supply chain delays. They decided they must bring the job back to the United States to eliminate it. One of the manufacturing employees took on the responsibility for leading this initiative. He brought together a team that included other manufacturing workers, equipment, and process engineers. They gathered inputs from other workers and created a specification for the equipment to do the job in the United States. The team took six months to nail down the scope and budget. They were able to bring the job in-house in nine months after the equipment was ready.

You can achieve feats like the above when you empower your teams. The employees collaborate to solve problems and derive immense satisfaction from doing so.

What Motivates Us?

Business leaders may believe that the only way to motivate their teams to excel is by giving them compensation, such as pay raises or perks. This belief overlooks the need for internal rewards in each of us. We have an intrinsic motivation that propels us to do a job well and experience the pride of accomplishment. In employee surveys, job satisfaction ranked very high. We possess an inner drive that wants us to do the job for a purpose beyond personal gain. We all want to know we are in control of our own lives, doing what we like to do in self-directed execution.

Leaders who are good at motivating their teams are aware of this intrinsic need and excel at empowerment. They started their journey by learning to delegate.

Empowering—The Process

Delegation doesn't come easy to most of us. The team leader and the members need to establish trust between themselves. Creating that trust is the first step in a relationship where delegation takes place. You can build this trust by being honest. Your team members see that there is no hidden agenda and that you are interested in their success. You state your expectations clearly. You show them you hold yourself to the same standards or higher that you expect of your team. When you make a mistake, take ownership and show humility. Show that you respect your team members and treat them with kindness and empathy. Create a culture that tolerates failure and allows a safe space for members to practice their craft.

In my software engineering career, I witnessed failures of many types. They could be software errors resulting in bugs seen after the system was in the hands of users. Design errors led to complete redesigns and wasted efforts during development. Managers who reported to me hired team members who were not good fits for the jobs or the culture. In all these cases, one mistake doesn't stop you from delegating. In our organization, we looked upon these occurrences as "teachable moments" and opportunities. We put systems and procedures in place to avoid mistakes.

The software development process comprises a series of failures. When a programmer writes code, seldom the code works for the first time. The assignment of code development includes "unit testing"[6] of the individual modules. The developers discover the errors and fix them before the next step of integrating the modules. "Unit tests" empower individual programmers to take ownership of their task—creation of the program. In another example, we identified why we hired an employee who was not a good fit. We discovered we were desperate to fill the position. We usually recruit multiple stakeholders to interview the candidate, but didn't in this case. A new procedure made it imperative that this will not happen in the future.

Learn to Empower

Figure 10.1 shows how empowerment relates to the skill level of the team member in decision-making.

Delegation is the lowest end of the delegation–empowerment continuum. The first step in learning to empower your team is to master delegation. When you delegate, you provide specifications for the task. You are not asking the team member to make any decisions but follow the directions and deliver the output as required. First-level managers

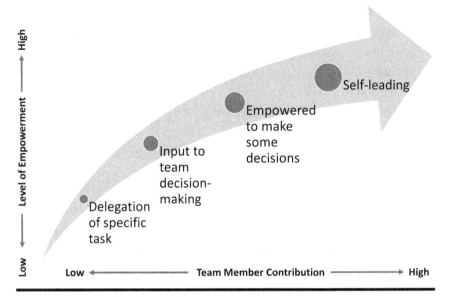

Figure 10.1 Delegation and empowerment.

with small teams must learn how to delegate well. As your career progresses, you will lead multiple teams whose managers report to you. You will find a mix of delegation and empowerment.

Imagine you are a newly promoted project leader. Your manager asks you to execute a project with the help of four or five team members. As a brand-new leader, you first need to learn how to handle your responsibilities, dividing the project into meaningful parts and assigning them to your project team. In leading your project, you keep tight control of your project since your responsibility is new. The team members may be new to you as well. You are yet to establish relationships and build mutual trust.

Delegating is not as simple as making someone responsible for a task, with some instructions and deadlines. When you are not fully aware of the capabilities of your team members, this is a recipe for disaster. Any time your team is brand new, the first step is to understand their capabilities.

The team may comprise senior and junior members. Find the limits of empowerment for each of them. If you realize a member is a candidate for delegation, come up with a plan to delegate. Monitor progress and remove roadblocks. Coach this member to increase her skill level so that you can empower her.

The growth in the empowerment process comes when you are comfortable asking your team member's input in decision-making. What brings on this comfort? You are now aware of the person's abilities, and you trust her to make informed decisions. There is a mutually workable relationship. Trust becomes a two-way street and collaboration can succeed.

At some point, your trust leads to making collaborative decisions. For example, you start a new project. You need to decide which team will have what responsibility of executing this project. Collaboration is required to make a decision involving all the team leaders. You acknowledge that the team leaders are knowledgeable, confident, and you trust their decisions enough to let them decide on their own for some limited scope of challenges. You have built mutual trust, confidence in each other, and shared values. When you are at a director level, you can now empower the managers in your team to take care of their team members.

The ultimate empowerment is the new leader who can carry on what you, as a leader, used to do. Perhaps now they can go beyond what you were capable of as a leader. That would be your proudest moment.

Train to Empower

What do you do if you find the task requires some training or coaching before you can delegate? Usually, you should be able to absorb the effort to do this in the task timeline. The training will help your team members grow, make your team's collective strength go up, and help you scale. You invest now for your future growth, as well as your team's. A fundamental principle behind delegation is to free yourself up for more value-added activities, which you can deliver better than your team members.

How do you support someone who is struggling with the task you delegated? The first step is to let him know your availability to help. Make sure he understands you are not looking to judge or criticize. The goal is to get the job done. Engage with him and listen actively. Guide his thinking to overcome the obstacles. You are acting as his coach and not his supervisor at this point. Use the coaching leadership style, which is to collaborate, support, and guide.

Don't Micromanage

We have all heard about micromanagers. A 2014 survey[7] found that 59% of employees had experience working for a micromanager. Of these, 55% reported their productivity was affected; 68% found the experience demoralizing. Micromanagers manage their team excessively, asking for every little detail. Every step requires their sign-off. They want constant assurance that the tasks are progressing well. If they learn about a misstep, they want to step in and correct the problem and are constantly worried that the team might let them down and spoil their reputation. Some of them are not even aware that they are doing it. Insecurity and low self-awareness are two of the primary reasons for this behavior.

Under micromanagers, team members show no initiative. They are disengaged. Micromanaging is the polar opposite of empowering. If you find yourself overworked and being a bottleneck, that is a clear sign you need to change. You can find help in your organization or guidance from a mentor in your network.

Some may think the opposite of micromanaging is to delegate and forget about it. As a leader, you own your team's execution. The delegated task is a shared responsibility. A leader who does not put in place milestones and periodic reviews is setting herself up for failure. Make team progress meetings an integral part of your tasks. Be sure to focus on the results and remove roadblocks. Be sure to praise the accomplishments. If you see the need for improvement, provide guidance. If the team needs training, take steps to provide it.

Framework for Empowering

Delegation is the first step in empowering your team, and those being empowered should have a mastery of needed skills.

But this is not sufficient. The following are the two other requirements for fostering empowerment (Figure 10.2):

■ Well-defined goals, missions, and strategies
■ A set of well-articulated and widely shared principles (or doctrines) embedded in the organizational culture

The first requirement says where to go, and the second says what are the fundamental beliefs as you make your way to the

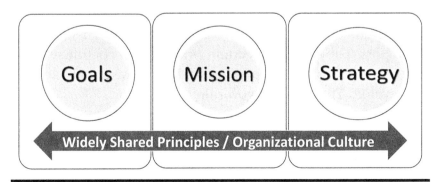

Figure 10.2   Empowerment framework.

goals. Most organizations are good at the art of expressing the first. It is harder to do the second.

Your team members want to know why they are doing what they do in their jobs. They get it when you talk about strategy and plans, but that information still doesn't tell them how their jobs relate to those. Your job as a leader is to bridge the gap between them. Business conditions change every day. They can change dramatically, as we saw when the COVID-19 pandemic hit. With such changes, there is no blueprint for how to do our jobs. We need to be flexible and adapt. We sure could use a framework that can help us. This framework comprises a code of conduct that says this is our culture, and we operate within these parameters. Empowerment gives everyone the autonomy to do what needs to be done, and the framework helps you stay true to the values. For example, think of yourself as a franchisor. Your team members are the franchisees. They run their businesses independently but have to abide by certain principles to uphold the brand. These principles form the framework in which the franchise operates. Similarly, anytime you use a distributed model of operation where the entities are autonomous, you need a framework for how it all comes together, applicable to your empowered team members.

In the software industry, many organizations possess high empowerment, for example, open-source software providers. Organizations such as Red Hat comprise many open-source developers. They abide by certain principles to contribute to the code repository. Communities such as these are highly empowered. They are self-governing.

Empowering Is Smart Leadership

As a leader, you may find the articulation of values easy. But if you don't model them in your behavior, you will find a mismatch. In decision-making, team members must have a good understanding of what needles they can move. Reinforce your values with appropriate rewards.

Make your team members autonomous. Help them understand how their work is relevant. Give them core principles to guide them. You will be a hero.

The smart way to create scale and endear yourself to your team is to empower them.

Practice

■ If you are a new manager, create a task list to delegate and train your team members. Make it part of your growth as a leader.

■ If you are a seasoned leader, review your activities in the past week. Could anyone in your team have taken over some of them? What can you do with your freed-up efforts?

■ Remind your team members their work makes a difference in achieving your goals.

Empowering—Questions to Ask Yourself

■ What am I doing to help my team grow?
■ What actions am I taking today that will multiply the leaders of my team?
■ Am I holding onto tasks that I can delegate? How does that affect my ability to add value?

Notes

1. Carnegie Advice, St. Louis Globe-Democrat, St. Louis, Missouri, October 15, 1899, p. 36, accessed September 24, 2021, https://www.newspapers.com/clip/84452036/carnegieadvice/.

2. "1997 Letter to Shareholders," Amazon.com, 1997, accessed June 14, 2021, https://www.sec.gov/Archives/edgar/data/1018724 /000119312516530910/d168744dex991.htm.

3. On the Greater Good, "The Truest Eye," *O Magazine*, accessed June 13, 2021, https://www.oprah.com/omagazine/Toni -Morrison-Talks-Love/4.

4. "About Gore," Gore.com, accessed September 20, 2021, https:// www.gore.com/about/the-gore-story.

5. About Gore. "Our Culture." Retrieved June 13, 2021, from https://www.gore.com/about/culture. Copyright ©2021, by W. L. Gore & Associates, Inc. Used by permission.

6. "Unit Testing," Wikipedia, accessed September 30, 2021, https:// en.wikipedia.org/wiki/Unit_testing.

7. "Survey: More than Half of Employees Have Worked for a Micromanager," *Cision PR Newswire*, July 01, 2014, accessed September 20, 2021, from https://www.prnewswire.com/news -releases/survey-more-than-half-of-employees-have-worked-for -a-micromanager-265359491.html.

Resources

Adam Grant, *Give and Take: Why Helping Others Drives Our Success* (Penguin Books, Kindle Edition, 2013).

Daniel H. Pink, *Drive: The Surprising Truth About What Motivates Us* (Riverhead Books, 2011).

Marty Cagan, *Empowered: Ordinary People, Extraordinary Products* (Wiley, 2020).

Simon Sinek, *Leaders Eat Last: Why Some Teams Pull Together and Others Don't* (Portfolio, 2014).

Chapter 11

All You Need Is Love

"All You Need Is Love" is a mantra that leaders should keep in their hearts to guide their followers. Gone are the days of dictatorial leaders. Today, enlightened leaders lead with their hearts and minds. This type of leadership is critical to growing and sustaining organizations with outstanding performance. In this chapter, we look at leaders who practice it. We describe strategies for leading with your heart. When you become such a leader, you are approachable and communicate with compassion and gratitude. You coach and empower your teams and build a culture that cares. You spread your love to your customers and other stakeholders.

About the Song

On June 25, 1967, a television special, a live and international satellite production called "One World,"

DOI: 10.4324/9781003267546-13   **151**

played this famous song for the first time. Parlophone released the song as a single the same year. It begins with a snippet from the French national anthem La Marseillaise and has a beautiful melody and a simple message that anyone can understand. Several artists covered "All You Need Is Love." Lennon and McCartney wrote this song during the height of the Vietnam war. John Lennon was the primary composer of the lyrics, which delivered a message that you can resolve everything with love. That is true for leadership as well.

All You Need Is Love—Heart-Led Leadership

Tenderness and kindness are not signs of weakness and despair, but manifestations of strength and resolution.

—Khalil Gibran[1]

What do you think of a culture that promotes love and individual creativity ?

In his book, *The Heart of Business: Leadership Principles for the Next Era of Capitalism,*[2] the former chair and CEO of Best Buy, Hubert Joly, tells the story of Jordan, a 3-year-old boy. His mother brought him to a Best Buy store in Florida with a broken dinosaur toy, a gift from "Santa Claus." The two sales associates she spoke to wanted to make the boy feel better. In any retail store, the sales associates would direct the customers to get a replacement. Instead, they enacted a play in which a doctor saves the dinosaur. They went through a mock medical procedure while exchanging the broken toy for a new one. Joly says no operating procedure could have taught the sales associates how to put a smile on a heartbroken kid. A blueprint for making a customer happy didn't exist. Best Buy's environment that appreciates an individual's creativity fostered this behavior and encouraged the sales associates to show their love for the customer.

Today's Leadership

Can you imagine a business leader speaking about love and work this way two or three decades ago? Leadership has undergone a lot of changes since the 1970s. Gone is the autocratic, my way or the highway style of leadership. In its place, we find leaders advocating a more collaborative, participative style of leadership that thrives on emotional intelligence and diversity. Changes in the business environment prompted some of this. Ten years ago, we expected the leaders to know everything and tell their organizations what to do and how to do it. We were used to a relatively stable environment. Today, the complexities brought on by technological advances, the global and connected workplace, and employees who have grown up with the internet and social media make collective wisdom the key to success. In this environment, leaders succeed by putting people first. They harness the power of their entire organization to bear and make things possible with their emotional intelligence. Today's successful leaders lead not by telling, but by listening and conversing. They lead by inspiring instead of by fear. Since early 2020, the coronavirus pandemic has created enormous challenges for leadership. We witness some outstanding leaders emerge during this challenging time. They lead with their hearts and minds.

Caring Leaders

Indra Nooyi, the former CEO of PepsiCo, is a leader who exemplifies the new leadership.

During a visit to India, her birthplace, she witnessed the many guests who came to her parents' house congratulating her mother on a job well done in raising a successful daughter. She realized how much her parents had contributed to her success, which led her to send letters to the parents of her team members, thanking them. She called out the impact the team members had on the success of the organization. The PepsiCo website[3] says Nooyi thanked the parents for gifting their child to the company.

Her unique act of gratitude prompted the parents to write back to her to say they were honored, and they shared their letters with friends, neighbors, and family. The team members were delighted and said this was the best thing that happened to their parents.

Nooyi's letters to her employees' parents did two important things—they made the employees feel appreciated and their families proud.

In 2015, Dan Price, the CEO of the payment processing company Gravity Payments,[4] increased the minimum salary of every employee in his company to $70,000 while decreasing his own salary from $1.1 million to that minimum. The experts expected Dan to fail in his business, but he proved the skeptics wrong. His employees amplified his behavior and made caring for each other and their customers their company culture.

During the coronavirus pandemic, several leaders showed the way to lead with compassion. Cisco Systems CEO Chuck Robbins and executive vice president Fran Katsoudas put people first and practiced compassion as the major thrust of their leadership.[5] In 2018, before the pandemic, Robbins emailed the employees with the subject "Making Mental Health a Priority." The response to this email from hundreds of employees led to having discussions about mental health, giving it equal importance as business topics. Cisco started offering mental health services to its employees and their children.

Jehangir Ratanji Dadabhoy (J.R.D.) Tata, the well-known leader of Tata Group in India, was a firm believer in leading with love. He had a fundamental requirement for a leader—leading humans with affection. He put people first.[6] When he chaired the Tata Group, any employee could write to him directly if they felt ill-treated.

Reliance Industries, one of the premier companies in India, showed what compassionate leadership is by instituting various measures such as continuing to provide salaries for five years to the nominee of employees who passed away because of the virus. They offered liberal time-off policies, financial help, and took care of the educational expenses of children whose parents passed away.

Heart-Led Leadership Messages

Mark Crowley, the author of *Lead from the Heart: Transformational Leadership for the 21st Century*[7] says that while the traditional leaders focused on driving performance and focused only on business goals, great leaders focus not only on performance but also on the needs of their workers, and work every day to improve their lives. When workers see this behavior of care and support, they reciprocate by doing their best for the organization.

In his doctoral dissertation, "To Lead is to Love: An Exploration into the Role of Love in Leadership,"[8] Dr. Joseph A. Ricciardi defines love as intimacy, passion, and commitment. He says:

> *In my opinion, it is love that makes people stand apart, that makes individuals into heroes, teams into champions, and memories. I will love and hope the reader does as well—those whom we lead deserve it.*

The paper "What's Love Got to Do with It? A Longitudinal Study of the Culture of Companionate Love and Employee and Client Outcomes in a Long-term Care Setting"[9] talks about love that one rarely associates with workplaces. Companionate love is about having deep affection and compassion for one another. It is about caring and having empathy. The authors of this paper set out to understand the impact of the culture of companionate love on work. Their study found that having companionate love at work positively affected the employees' well-being. They had more job satisfaction, reduced absenteeism, and burnout.

William Vincent Campbell Jr., or Bill Campbell, as he is known, was the head football coach at Columbia University, CEO of Go, Claris, and Intuit, chair of the board of Intuit, and the board of trustees of Columbia University. He coached many business leaders, including Steve Jobs of Apple and Google's Eric Schmidt. The book *Trillion Dollar Coach*[10] immortalized him. When the authors of this book discussed Bill with their interviewees, they were surprised to hear the word love used so many times. They say Bill created a culture of companionate love by caring deeply about the lives of those he worked and interacted with. He had no hesitation showing his love for those he cared about at work and outside of work.

The leadership trend is clear—the way to success is through the heart.

Leading Your Team with Love

How do you love your team members? There are many things you can do to show that you care for them. Here are a few successful strategies to get you started (Figure 11.1).

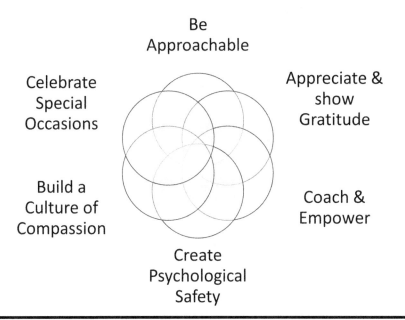

Be
Approachable

Celebrate
Special
Occasions

Appreciate &
show
Gratitude

Build a
Culture of
Compassion

Coach &
Empower

Create
Psychological
Safety

Figure 11.1   Heart-Led strategies.

Appreciate and Show Gratitude

The O.C. Tanner Institute and HealthStream conducted a study in the United States and Canada with 100,000 participants. This study showed 79% of employees who quit their jobs gave "lack of appreciation" as the main reason for their decision to leave.[11] Over 90% of those with excellent morale reported their managers were good at recognizing their work. Heartfelt communication with your team is one of the most important things you can do. Tell them what difference they make to the success of the group. When you see someone doing something exceptionally well, give kudos in front of the entire team. When a team member shares a success, use the opportunity. Create a connection by asking them to tell you how they accomplished it. As a leader, you can help the team members connect the dots. Teach them about how their work is meaningful to the team and the entire organization. For example, if a programmer created a tool to speed up the build time during software development, measure the impact on the team's productivity, and praise the programmer with that measurable impact. Be genuine and be specific. Thank them, a habit I developed early in my leadership that I continue today. No matter how crazy my day is, I always take a minute to say thank you. Show your team you value their opinions and ideas by thanking them when the accomplishment is fresh in your mind.

You create a sense of belonging among your team members when you acknowledge the individual contributions of the members. Through your actions, you can help the team members feel connected to you and one another. The team members can see how their contributions help achieve the common goals. Showing you are an inclusive leader who values diversity galvanizes the entire team to adopt this mindset.

Be Approachable

Connect with the team members every chance you get. Walk around the office and have a casual conversation. Meet with them in regular one-on-one meetings. Or, you could go out for coffee, or lunch, or take a walk. I used to arrive at the office quite early in the day, one of the first few to do so. I still remember some conversations with team members when I grabbed a cup of coffee as they started their work-day, which resulted in solving some complex problems at work. Sometimes it helped me understand personal issues they were encountering and help them. Even during the pandemic, when we are working remotely, you can still have informal communication through the wonders of technology—Slack, Teams, instant messaging. Grab the opportunity when you see it. Be available and practice an open-door policy. Let the team members understand you are available to them and that you are approachable. You do this by initiating conversations and being responsive. When a team member reaches out to you with a question, you may not have an answer. You may need time to think about it. Tell him immediately you are listening and set up a time to discuss later.

Coach and Empower

Your team has aspirations. Be their champion. Empower them to express themselves. When you see something that is not aligned with your original thinking, don't discredit it. Develop a habit of asking, "Can you tell me more?" which is an excellent way to show you care. You show your love by listening actively and being genuine. There will be times when you see unacceptable performance or behaviors. Don't wait to talk about it. Give your constructive feedback for course correction and coach them to do better.

Create Psychological Safety

Amy Edmondson, Professor of Leadership and Management at the Harvard Business School, introduced team psychological safety as "a shared belief held by members of a team that the team is safe for interpersonal risk-taking."[12] Your team members should feel that they are in a safe space on your team. Team members must feel secure in taking calculated risks and fail. It is essential that each of them knows it is ok to bring up tough conversations expecting to have honest discussions about them and feel comfortable bringing up conflicts. Every team member must show an attitude of helping each other and believe that they can bring their entire self to work with you and the rest of the team. A leader who provides this psychological safety sets up her team for success, growth, and happiness.

Build a Culture of Compassion

"Culture" has its origin in the Latin word "cultus," which has many meanings. Care is one of them. As a leader, express your love, concern, and compassion for your team members, and the culture of compassion will develop. If you are caring, each team member will learn to care for others on the team. Canva.com is an Australian company whose online tool empowers everyone anywhere in the world to design anything and publish anywhere. Their blog on kindness in the workplace[13] is a testament to their cultural values. Inspire your team to build a culture of kindness. Every member you hire in your team has to contribute to the overall culture and philosophy. Hire a job candidate not only because she has demonstrable abilities to do the job. Offer her the position because she is a great cultural fit.

Learn to care for your team in every way possible to achieve team goals and their physical and mental well-being. Once I drove one of my team members who experienced a

Remember the scare my son gave me when I was near end of my preg with him at CSIM? Instead of calling 911, you took me to the hospital in your own van and stayed with me until my husband arrived! Thank you so much for your caring heart, Shantha! 💜 I always remember that throughout the years, even though I don't see you. 🩶🩶

I don't expect you to remember that incident either. You are a kind person. The things that you usually do probably seem normal and insignificant to you, but they do touch people's hearts and people do appreciate your doings. Here's one more doing that you probably don't remember — after that incident, you let me work from home to take care of my pregnancy until giving birth. Your book talked about giving wings to women with career. You did give me and other people wings, Shantha! To balance our career and home life. You gave me wings. And all others under your management as well. You guided us and let us learned and grow. You were a good manager, Shantha. No, a great manager!

    I sometimes feel that you were like a mom to all of us, even though you're not that much older. 😊💜💜

Figure 11.2   Note of thanks.

scare during her pregnancy to the hospital. She remembered this even after two decades. She messaged and told me her son is now a full-fledged graduate student. You can imagine how motivated she would have been in the team's success and helped achieve its goals. Figure 11.2 depicts her own words.

Celebrate Special Occasions

There are ways to show how much you love your team. Greetings on holidays and parties on special occasions, such as achieving a specific goal, are some ways to say you love them. In the company I cofounded, we held holiday parties for the employees and spouses. There were toasts to the spouses, thanking them for their support in making the company successful. We acknowledged that there were times during which the employees put work ahead of family. The company celebrated birthdays together for several team members who were born in the same month.

How to Love Your Customers

Loving your customers begins with showing your employees love. A much-loved employee will care for customers, creating a multiplier effect. Train and develop your staff so that they can become competent in how they serve the customers. If your culture fosters compassion, this will extend to your customers, partners, and other stakeholders.

Your customers buy your products or services because they need them. Address the customers' needs as expected, with excellent quality. If you have a business delivering a project, be sure to honor the time and budget commitments.

Listen to your customers. Use their feedback to make your products and services better. There may be times when you may not like what you see. Exercise patience and rectify the situation.

Thank your customers for supporting your business. Always be honest in your dealings with them. Be upfront about an expected issue with your product or service. Treat your customers as your champions and give them visibility in the industry every chance you get.

While you are wooing new customers with promotions, don't forget your loyal customers. Many businesses have loyalty programs. Be sure to institute one.

Heart and Head Together Build Performance

This chapter focused on heart-led leadership. Leaders who practice it don't forget what their heads tell them about the business excellence of growth, revenue, and profits. Every heart-led action actually helps with the bottom line. When you take care of your team, the effect multiplies to include your team's results, business, customers, and stakeholders.

In his book *Excellence Now: Extreme Humanism*,[14] Tom Peters, whom I admire for his message, "people first," and for his staunch advocacy of women's leadership, says:

> *Take care of people—train them and treat them with kindness and respect and help them prepare for tomorrow. Insist that every employee commit to encouraging growth and caring for their mates. This goes double—or triple—in today's troubled times. The goal is Extreme Employee Engagement (E-cubed). The bottom line is to make excellence the norm in all people matters. (The 'bottom line' is also that this is the best way to grow and the best spur to profitability.)*

The road to success is putting people first.

Practice

- Take a team member out on her birthday for lunch.
- Write a thank-you note to your team member's family.
- Practice informal communication.

Heart-Led Leadership — Questions to Ask Yourself

- How often do I get out there among my team members and engage in casual conversations?
- Do I listen more than I talk?
- Do I understand my customers? When did I speak to one last?

Notes

1. Khalil Gibran, *The Kahlil Gibran Reader: Inspirational Writings* (Copyright: Philosophical Library, Kensington Publishing Corporation, 2006).
2. Hubert Joly, *The Heart of Business: Leadership Principles for the Next Era of Capitalism* (Harvard Business Review Press, 2021).
3. "PepsiCo: Power of Thank You Letters," *lovetoappreciate.com* , January 16, 2018, accessed September 24, 2021, https://www .lovetoappreciate.com/pepsico-power-thank-you-letters/.
4. "Dan Price," Wikipedia, June 1, 2021, accessed June 4, 2021, https://en.wikipedia.org/wiki/Dan_Price.
5. Andrew Marquardt, "Putting People First: Cisco CEO on Leading through a Year of Unprecedented Hardship," *Forune .com*, February 25, 2021, accessed June 10, 2021, https://fortune .com/2021/02/25/cisco-ceo-chuck-robbins-leadership-covid -pandemic/.
6. Arun Maira, "JRD Tata — The Democratic Capitalist," *The Hindu Business Line*, May 23, 2020, accessed June 19, 2021, https://www.thehindubusinessline.com/opinion/jrd-tata-the -democratic-capitalist/article31652225.ece.
7. Mark C. Crowley, *Lead from the Heart: Transformational Leadership for the 21st Century* (Balboa Press, 2011).

8. Joseph A. Ricciardi, "To Lead Is to Love: An Exploration into the Role of Love in Leadership," a dissertation submitted to Benedictine University, May 2014.
9. Sigal G. Barsade & Olivia A. O'Neill, "What's Love Got to Do with It? A Longitudinal Study of the Culture of Companionate Love and Employee and Client Outcomes in a Long-Term Care Setting," *Administrative Science Quarterly*, Vol. 59, No. 4 (December 2014): 551–598. https://doi.org/10.1177/0001839214538636.
10. Eric Schmidt, Jonathan Rosenberg, & Alan Eagle, *Trillion Dollar Coach* (Harper Business, 2019).
11. David Sturt & Todd Nordstrom, "The Evolution of the Manager ... And What It Means for You," *Forbes: Careers*, September 11, 2014, accessed June 25, 2021, https://www.forbes.com/sites/davidsturt/2014/09/11/the-evolution-of-the-manager-and-what-it-means-for-you/.
12. Amy C. Edmondson, "Psychological Safety and Learning Behavior in Work Teams," Johnson Graduate School of Management, Cornell University, *Administrative Science Quarterly*, Vol. 44, No. 2 (June 1999): 350–383, accessed June 21, 2021, https://journals.sagepub.com/doi/10.2307/2666999.
13. Jennie Rogerson, "The Importance of Being Kind at Work," *Canva Team*, April 22, 2021, accessed June 18, 2021, https://medium.com/canva/the-importance-of-being-kind-at-work-774d144418aa.
14. Tom Peters, *Excellence Now: Extreme Humanism* (Networlding Publishing, 2021).

Resources

Amy C. Edmondson, *The Fearless Organization: Creating Psychological Safety in the Workplace for Learning, Innovation, and Growth* (Wiley, 2018).
Daniel Coyle, *The Culture Code: The Secrets of Highly Successful Groups* (Bantam, 2018).
Mark C. Crowley, *Lead from the Heart: Transformational Leadership for the 21st Century* (Balboa Press, 2011).
Tom J. Peters, *Excellence Now: Extreme Humanism* (Networlding Publishing, 2021).

LEADERSHIP
MASTERY

3

Chapter 12

I've Got a Feeling

How many times have you trusted a feeling that has no logical explanation? We call that intuition or gut feeling. When used under certain conditions, intuition is a powerful tool in a leader's arsenal. All of us experience situations where our guts tell us what to do. Many leaders acknowledge they rely on intuition occasionally in decision-making. Even skeptics agree that in some cases, you must go with your intuition. In getting help from experts and trusting their intuition, leaders need to be convinced of their domain knowledge. The chapter suggests guidelines for using intuition.

About the Song

Released in 1970 as a song in the album *Let It Be*, "I've Got a Feeling" combined two unfinished segments. The introductory part, written by Paul

DOI: 10.4324/9781003267546-15

McCartney, is a love song about his future wife Linda and is the title. John's contribution starts with lamenting a challenging year, reflecting the low point in his life, his divorce from his wife, Cynthia. Irrespective of what the lyrics say, the words remind me of the power of intuition.

I've Got a Feeling—Using Intuition

*When you have no data, let your intuition guide you.
It has served me well.*

The Beatle, Paul McCartney, the accepted writer of the song, "Yesterday," had a dream in which he heard a tune that he believed was magical. At the same time, he felt that this song sounded very different from the typical songs created by the band. He thought it probably wouldn't do well among the fans and critics. But his intuition told him to go with it, and thus was born one of the most successful songs of all time.

A Personal Narrative—Estimation and Intuition

As a software engineering leader, the one significant problem I faced throughout my career was estimating the amount of effort required to develop software. We see a lot of discussion about this in the software development literature. We mistakenly believe we don't need estimates if we use agile methods. A recent paper[1] makes the case why it is more important now more than ever to estimate efforts in software development. The reasons for poor effort estimation are many. For example, you had never used the tools involved. Or, some engineers are new to the team and haven't quite gotten into the rhythm. Or, the estimates don't account for the bugs one discovers in some third-party or open-source software. The list goes on.

A project comprising many pieces of software has its effort estimated by combining the individual estimates. Many of these components depend on other pieces being available. The result is the delivery schedule of a software system or functionality that is a highly inaccurate forecast, costing the organization goodwill with customers and, often, loss of revenue. While my experience has been with software development, we see this in all planning tasks, the "planning fallacy" proposed by Kahneman and Tversky.[2] It says how bad we humans are in estimating how long it takes to complete a task. Early in my career, I was an optimistic engineer. But I learned over time to not only temper my optimism, but to spot an underestimation coming from my team members the minute I saw it. I could also identify an overestimation from someone who was not a productive team member, which allowed me to question the estimate and get better ones, not only for the development we knew how to do, but for those projects we never did before. What I was doing was applying my intuition or gut reaction.

It Feels Right

Merriam-Webster[3] defines intuition as follows:

1a: the power or faculty of attaining to direct knowledge or cognition without evident rational thought and inference
 b: immediate apprehension or cognition
 c: knowledge or conviction gained by intuition

2: quick and ready insight

What do you do when you encounter a situation that is nothing like what you saw before and there is no data? How about those complex situations where you have collected a lot of data but your gut instinct says you would be wrong to decide purely based on the data available? What about those situations where you need to make a snap decision? How do you do it?

You use your intuition, sometimes called gut reaction.

Creative people use intuition all the time, just like Paul McCartney did with the song "Yesterday." In complex situations, you need creativity to go beyond what any available data may tell you.

We are aware of several intuitive leaders. Henry Ford of the Ford Motor Company was one of them, who doubled the wages of his workers in 1914. Apparently, he "felt" doing this was right and also had a few other insights. Ford predicted that this would attract more reliable workers who would be able to handle the pressure and monotony of the assembly line, and he was right! Among modern leaders, Bill Gates is known to talk about situations where we are forced to rely on intuition in decision-making. We have heard Steve Jobs say that your intuition can tell you what you should become, and you must apply the courage to follow it.

The Intelligence of the Unconscious Mind

We may perceive intuition as something unexplainable. However, this is actually the result of our experiences over the years. Intuition is the accumulation of all the insights gathered in the past and the wisdom we gained from all the talented people we meet over the years of living. It is the collection of facts and data in our memories.

Wikipedia says, "Fingerspitzengefühl" is a German term, literally meaning "fingertips feeling," showing intuitive flair or instinct. The English language adopted this as a loanword, and it describes a great situational awareness and the ability to respond most appropriately and tactfully. Complex situations and problems require such understanding. When we need to handle delicate situations, those with fingertip feelings can do so with tact. During a soccer game, Dutch-American football coach Thomas Rongen said the professional soccer player Christian Pulisic has Fingerspitzengefühl. He said Pulisic has a unique, intuitive feel for the game.

Several researchers[4] set out to prove a hypothesis named "deliberation-without-attention." This hypothesis says conscious deliberation may work for simple situations. However, unconscious thought is involved when making complex decisions, such as buying a car or house. Four studies involved in purchasing complex products confirmed this hypothesis. You are better off deciding unconsciously when a lot of information needs to be considered. In other words, use your intuition.

Colin Powell is a retired four-star general and was the first African-American US Secretary of State, serving between 2001 and 2005. In his book *My American Journey*,[5] he describes his decision-making philosophy. Powell says he gets as much information as he can on the problem. Then he uses his instinct to test what they tell him. Since you cannot wait indefinitely to decide, he came up with a formula. If he perceives the information gives him only a 40% chance of making the right decision, he continues to gather information. He doesn't wait for that chance to be 100%. The range that works for him is somewhere between 40% and 70%.

Gerd Gigerenzer is a psychologist. He is also the director emeritus of the Center for Adaptive Behavior and Cognition (ABC) at Max Planck Institute for Human Development in Berlin. An interviewer[6] asked him about the role of intuition and gut feelings in business, and Gerd answered gut feelings are tools based on substantial experience. He said they are forms of intelligence of the unconscious mind. In his experience of working with large companies, he found they made important decisions 50% of the time based on gut feelings.

System 1 and System 2 Thinking

In his book *Thinking, Fast and Slow*,[7] Daniel Kahneman explains the two-systems approach to judgment and choice.

System 1 describes the thinking when no effort is involved. For example, when you view a beautiful landscape, you immediately experience joy. The thought is fast, unconscious, and automatic. We don't control System 1 thinking. We sense it, and it is passive.

System 2 describes the slow thinking , where effort is involved. It is conscious, deliberate, and controlled. For example, in deciding how much to spend during my shopping, I consider what I can afford, and the limit on my spending.

Usually, most of what we think starts with System 1 thinking, which prompts System 2 thinking when making hard decisions. In the example of shopping, System 2 thinking kicks in when buying an expensive or complex product. If I see a pack of gum, I may buy that without too much thought. System 1 thinking is intuitive. System 2 thinking is logical.

Kahneman says intuition functions very well for the most part.[8] He says when the domain is reasonably predictable, and you have extensive experience, it can work.

In a *McKinsey Quarterly* interview,[9] Kahneman and psychologist Gary Klein (who pioneered naturalistic decision-making) discussed the merits of intuition for business leaders. Kahneman's position is that you can trust your intuition under certain conditions, such as when you are under time pressure to make a decision. However, there are some caveats. Overconfidence often renders an intuitive approach to decision-making wrong. Inexperience in the domain of problem-solving makes intuitive decisions suspect. Applying familiar patterns learned unconsciously to unrelated situations makes intuition unreliable.

Intuition Is Recognition

The Nobel Laureate Herb Simon defines intuition as recognition. In his 1991 Keynote Address to the Third Annual

Convention of the American Psychological Society,[10] he describes a scene where three Tamil women discuss cooking. One woman is an expert in cooking. One of the other two women asks the expert how long it takes to cook a specific dish in the oven. The expert answers that she doesn't use any *"systematic rules"* and that she uses her experience. Simon says we employ the word intuition to describe behavior such as this. We use it to answer questions without clear reasoning. The expert finds a cue in the situation, accessing the answer from the memory storage. Simon says that intuition is nothing more than recognition, and precisely that. As someone who has been cooking for a long time, the story resonates with me. The street conversation might have easily been between my daughter and me.

When and How to Use Intuition—Be Conscious of Your Knowns and Unknowns

All of us are born with the ability to make intuitive decisions. When we gain experience in what we do, our brain stores away the insights we derive from them. We bring up these insights when we encounter a similar situation. We may not always be consciously aware of how we possess this knowledge. All that said, applying intuition to leadership decision-making requires understanding the limitations of our intuitive competence.

The mental model "Circle of Competence"[11] attributed to Warren Buffett and Charlie Munger says that experts garner a lot of knowledge but may be overconfident of what they actually possess (Figure 12.1). In making a decision intuitively, if the experts go beyond their circle of competence, it is likely that such a decision is not trustworthy. To trust your intuitive judgment, you need to be aware of what you know and what you don't know and be very conscious of it.

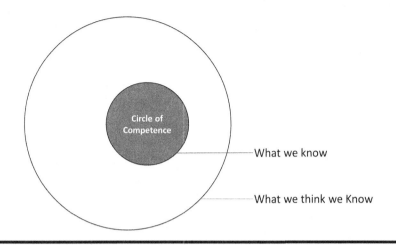

Figure 12.1   Circle of competence.

In an article about experts,[12] the authors talk about how they seem to solve problems intuitively. If business leaders can understand why some experts operate the way they do, this understanding can help find them and cultivate their contributions to the business.

Guidelines for Leaders

Here are some guidelines for leaders in applying intuition:

- If you are in a situation that you can analyze with data to arrive at an answer, use this approach. Even after seeing the insights from the data, sometimes you are sure about your gut feelings. If so, you would want to listen to your inner voice.
- Intuition is valuable when we face a situation that requires an immediate decision. When there is not much data for analysis, you have no choice but to rely on it.
- Don't trust intuition if you possess absolutely no experience in a particular domain or field. Instead, rely on

someone who is an expert in the area, and temper her recommendation with personal judgment, such as asking: Is the expert overconfident?

■ When you come up with an intuitive answer, do not blindly follow it. Look at the decision and deliberate to understand if it fits the context.

■ If you cannot get immediate feedback on your decision, it is hard to validate your gut instincts and refine them.

■ Whether you use your intuition or the intuitions of the experts you rely on, understand the circle of competence involved. If the competency is outside of that circle, the decision is untrustworthy. Which means you must understand the experts working with you. Do your due diligence, talk to those with experience in using the expert and the context.

■ Do a premortem. A 1989 research found that premortem increases the ability to identify reasons correctly for future outcomes by 30%.[13] Imagine the decision turns out to be wrong and ask what could be the reasons (inversion is a great critical thinking skill to develop).[14]

For those uncomfortable with trusting their intuition, recognition-primed decision (RPD) model, which combines System 1 level thinking with a System 2 level capability, can be helpful.

Recognition-Primed Decision Model

Gary Klein published the RPD model[15] in 1993 to help overcome limitations of analytical decision-making under challenging conditions with time pressure, such as in a hospital emergency care, war, and firefighting (Figure 12.2). This model is of great help to those with considerable experience (ten years or more) when little data is available for using analytical methods. Two elements comprise the RPD model. The first

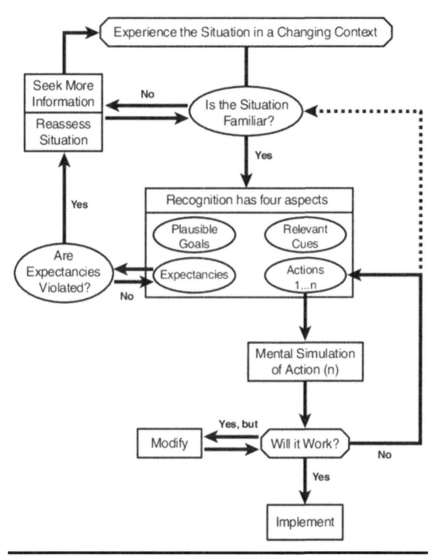

Figure 12.2 A recognition-primed decision (RPD) model of rapid decision-making by G.A. Klein, 1993.

one is analogous to Kahneman's System 1—fast and intuitive pattern-matching. The second is analogous to System 2—a deliberate and conscious mental activity to evaluate what the first element came up with.

The decision-maker considers the situation and asks herself whether the case is familiar, something she has encountered before, the recognition aspect of the model. The recognition involves understanding the cues that lead to pattern matching and choosing a course of action, the first element of the RPD model. Using mental models accumulated through experience, the decision-maker then plays out the course of action in her mind. This "mental simulation of action" is the second element of the RPD model.

Since RPD is primed with intuition, all the guidelines of how to use intuition mentioned earlier apply.

Intuition Is a Powerful Tool

Intuitions, or gut feelings, are highly valuable in leadership decision-making under certain conditions, based on leadership anecdotes and scientific studies. All leaders can learn to use their intuition with caution and practice. RPD is an excellent tool when used appropriately. As you progress in your leadership journey, intuition will help you deal with situations where analytical help is not available.

Practice

- Every day, set aside time to reflect on what your intuition said about a situation before you applied analysis to it. You might not have acted on the instinct, but capture it. Keep track of how you felt when you first thought about it, and how the decision played out.
- Track your team project's planning tasks, their initial estimates, and the actuals. Train your team members to become better at estimating their jobs by conducting a postmortem on this data.

- Do a premortem on an upcoming project to identify everything that can go wrong and what you can do about it.
- Mindfulness helps grow your intuition. Learn to live mindfully by conscious practice.

Using Intuition—Questions to Ask Yourself

- How big a part intuition plays in my decision-making?
- How do I increase my ability to make decisions when under time pressure?

Notes

1. Larry Putnam Jr., "Why Software Estimation Is More Important Now than Ever," *InfoQ*, March 8, 2018, accessed July 1, 2021, https://www.infoq.com/articles/software-estimation-important/.
2. Daniel Kahneman & Amos Tversky, "Intuitive Prediction: Biases and Corrective Procedures," *TIMS Studies in Management Science*, Vol. 12 (1979): 313–327.
3. "Intuition," Merriam-Webster Dictionary, accessed June 9, 2021, https://www.merriam-webster.com/dictionary/intuition.
4. Ap Dijksterhuis, et al., "On Making the Right Choice: The Deliberation-without-Attention Effect," *Science*, Vol. 311, No. 5763 (2006): 1005–1007, accessed June 9, 2021, https://doi.org/10.1126/science.1121629.
5. Colin L. Powell & Joseph E. Persico, *My American Journey* (Random House, 1995).
6. Justin Fox, "Instinct Can Beat Analytical Thinking," *Harvard Business Review*, June 20, 2014, accessed June 9, 2021, https://hbr.org/2014/06/instinct-can-beat-analytical-thinking.
7. Daniel Kahneman, *Thinking, Fast and Slow* (Farrar, Straus and Giroux, 2011).
8. SPIEGEL Interview with Daniel Kahneman, "Debunking the Myth of Intuition," *Spiegel International*, May 25, 2012, accessed June 9, 2021, https://www.spiegel.de/international/zeitgeist/interview-with-daniel-kahneman-on-the-pitfalls-of-intuition-and-memory-a-834407.html.

9. *McKinsey Quarterly* Interview, "Strategic Decisions: When Can You Trust Your Gut?" McKinsey Company, May 25, 2012, accessed June 9, 2021, https://www.mckinsey.com/business -functions/strategy-and-corporate-finance/our-insights/strategic -decisions-when-can-you-trust-your-gut.

10. Herbert A. Simon, "What Is an Explanation of Behavior?" *Psychological Science*, Vol. 3 (1992): 150–161.

11. "Circle of Competence," Wikipedia, October 26, 2020, accessed June 16, 2021, https://en.wikipedia.org/wiki/Circle_of _competence.

12. Michael J. Prietula & Herbert A. Simon, "The Experts in Your Midst," *Harvard Business Review*, 1989, accessed June 9, 2021, https://hbr.org/1989/01/the-experts-in-your-midst.

13. Gary Klein, "Performing a Project Premortem," *Harvard Business Review*, September 2007, accessed June 9, 2021, https://hbr.org/2007/09/performing-a-project-premortem.

14. James Clear, "Inversion: The Crucial Thinking Skill Nobody Ever Taught You," *Jamesclear.com*, accessed June 9, 2021, https://jamesclear.com/inversion

15. Gary A. Klein, "A Recognition-Primed Decision (RPD) Model of Rapid Decision Making," in Gary A. Klein, Judith Orasanu, Roberta Calderwood, Caroline E. Zsambok (eds.) *Decision Making in Action: Models and Methods* (Ablex Publishing, 1993), 138–147.

Resources

Daniel Kahneman, *Thinking, Fast and Slow* (Farrar, Straus and Giroux, 2011).
Gary Klein, *The Power of Intuition: How to Use Your Gut Feelings to Make Better Decisions at Work* (Currency, 2004).

Chapter 13

Hello, Goodbye

The quintessential opposite words—hello and goodbye—coming and going, remind me that leadership
is all about balancing the opposites, the tensions that
occur when leading. A skilled leader understands
the situation and manages the tensions involved. She
navigates with leadership personas that range from
visionary, to coach, to democratic, to the affiliate. She
uses the pacesetting and coercive leadership styles
with great restraint. This chapter looks at leaders who
have handled tensions well and the different situational leadership styles.

About the Song

The Beatles recorded "Hello, Goodbye" in October
and released it in November 1967. Paul wrote it,
though, like many other songs, it is credited to
Lennon-McCartney. It was a chart-topper in most

DOI: 10.4324/9781003267546-16

of the countries. Apparently, John did not like the song and called it meaningless. His "I am the Walrus" is the B-side of this song on A-side, and was perhaps another reason for his dislike. Paul wrote the song when meeting with an assistant of The Beatles' manager, asking for opposites to the words he came up with such as stop for go, yes for now, and hello for goodbye. Paul usually takes an optimistic point of view in most of the songs. This song proved no different. He talks about the deep theme of duality in the universe in his biography *Many Years from Now*.[1]

Hello, Goodbye—Balancing the Tensions

Tensions are inevitable on your leadership journey.
Take them as opportunities to learn and grow.

A leader must recognize that while she may be an expert in some areas, she needs help in other realms, and must become a learner. She needs to understand that time-tested strategies work in some situations, but in the fast-changing world, you need new solutions. Exemplary leaders know when to talk and when to shut up and listen. They are aware of when to exercise authority and when to share it. Savvy leaders understand when and how to use intuition and analytics in decision-making. They comprehend the balance between having perfection versus having a good enough approach.

The universe comprises opposing forces, and leadership is similar. Opposing forces create tensions and exceptional leaders understand every action has its pros and cons. They have learned to balance them.

Balance is also key to the everyday behavior of leaders. On the one hand, you want to give your team confidence in your leadership, but how can you express confidence without coming across as arrogant? How can you be authentic while adapting the lessons of other leaders? As a leader, how do you set a pace for execution while comprehending the individuality of your team members? When you show you care about those you lead, how do you do it without letting them take advantage of it?

Challenges for the New and Experienced Leaders

If you are a newly promoted manager, you will experience one of the most challenging tensions in your leadership journey. You are exceptional at what you do as an individual contributor. Your boss recognizes your value and promotes you to be the team manager. Now you need to lead an entire team to contribute to your organization. I learned to manage this hard tension when I first got promoted several decades ago. The need to step away from the mentality of "my accomplishments" to "our accomplishments" created one problem. Another issue was doing things my way versus bringing out the best in my team members to achieve success for the entire team. I also experienced the tension between the attention to tasks completion and the team members' satisfaction in their work and their learning.

Later, in my career as the head of software engineering, I saw plenty of opportunities to practice the yin and the yang of leadership. We encountered a challenge selling our flagship product to new industries. In a classic case of a square peg being pushed into a round hole, the product was not a great fit for them. We had an R&D effort to create a new version of the product that appeared to be going nowhere. Our existing customers resisted the use of an unproven product. A few of us proposed that the recent version should address the new market. We can continue to develop the current product with next-generation capabilities. Since I led the engineering team of the flagship product, I executed the plan. Under my leadership, we brought out new generations of products addressing the current customers, which helped customer satisfaction.

Fair treatment of team members also creates tensions. For example, a leadership style that doesn't consider cultural differences in global team members will fail. When I led teams in the United States, China, and India, I needed to account for the variation in work habits. In China, the team members needed the freedom to take a short afternoon siesta, not a practice followed by other offices. Organizations have ignored the fair treatment of women for a long time. For example, a female team member who is a mother may appreciate having flexible hours more than getting a membership at a golf club. You can navigate these tensions by acknowledging each of us is unique.

A Modern-Day Leader

Leaders have to show empathy for those they lead while bolstering their spirits to keep going. During the COVID-19 pandemic, we have seen a few leaders handle this with aplomb. For example, *The Atlantic* magazine carried an article on April 19, 2020,[2] praising the actions of the New Zealand Prime Minister Jacinda Ardern. It called out how unique she is in her leadership, full of empathy, encouraging people to care for themselves in a crisis. The article pointed to her clear and consistent communication, while serious, is also full of compassion. A former prime minister said people appreciate that she is not preaching to them but is standing with them. They put their lives in her hands even when they don't quite understand all the actions. They trust her completely.

Another quote from a scholar said she doesn't blame others, gives positive vibes, and manages expectations. The article noted that Ardern's leadership style—portraying herself as one of those she leads—is interesting, if nothing else. Still, it is remarkable because she combines her style with policies that produce outstanding results.

You can manage leadership tensions (Figure 13.1) using different strategies. In Chapter 12, "I've Got a Feeling," I explain when to use intuition and when to use analytical methods. Chapter 5, "Help!" describes how to ask for help when you need it. Chapters on lifelong learning, leading with humility, and thinking for yourself can all be helpful.

Leadership Tensions

Strategic Thinking	Operational Thinking
Leading	Learning
Telling	Listening
Authoritarian	Democratic
Analytical	Intuitive
Perfection	Good enough
Confidence	Humility
Motivating	Empathetic
Kind	Candid
Task oriented	People Oriented

Figure 13.1   Leadership tensions.

Tensions and Teams

I follow Tom Peters,[3] author of several books, including In *Search of Excellence*, on Twitter. He recently posted some tweets[4] (Figure 13.2).

When I replied to these tweets, I said: "The yin and the yang."

Peters mentioned many more of the tensions in his tweets: being kind versus being candid; the attitude that you are doing your job versus appreciating the extra effort; communicating to get things done versus communicating to develop a relationship; and staying in the corner office versus mixing with the front-line team members. How successful you are as a leader depends on how well you handle them.

Tom Peters ✅
@tom_peters

···

You like strategy. I like execution. You like big gestures.
I like small gestures. You worry about disruption. I
worry about the next five minutes. You like systems. I
like people. You like to "tell it like it is." I like kindness.
···

10:11 AM · May 11, 2021 · Twitter for iPad

Tom Peters ✅
@tom_peters

···

Replying to @tom_peters

You like "It's your job." I like "Thanks for the extra
effort." You like to "get down to business." I like to see
how folks are doing. You like your office. I like the shop
floor. You like people "who get to the point." I like
people who think before they open their mouth.

10:16 AM · May 11, 2021 · Twitter for iPad

Figure 13.2   Tom Peters' tweets on leadership challenges.

Skilled leaders don't see themselves only as task-oriented
or people-oriented. Instead, they are constantly evaluating
the situation and applying their best judgment that fits. These
leaders balance the need to be strong and lead the way by
empowering the team that can lead itself. They understand
their strengths but also see their weaknesses and work to
compensate them.

The contradictory forces, when combined, can create a
powerful approach to leadership. Today's leaders recognize
that they need to balance between the tensions and use a
diverse team to accomplish extraordinary results. An excellent
leader is very good at managing the tensions that arise when
working with her team.

Managing Team Leadership Tensions

As mentioned earlier, leadership tensions are challenging when you are working with your team. You can manage such tensions well with situational leadership.

Situational leadership involves flexibility and adaptability. The leader changes the style of leadership to suit the situation. A situational leader moves from one leadership style to another to meet the growing needs of an organization and its stakeholders. She uses her insights to tune her approach, depending on the situation. She understands what leadership strategy fits each new paradigm she encounters.

Author and journalist, Daniel Goleman,[5] defines six styles within situational leadership in leading teams—visionary, coaching, democratic, affiliative, pacesetting, and coercive. Others classify leadership styles into eight types, some of which overlap with Goleman's six styles. What is essential is that situational leaders flex their style of leading to fit what they encounter. Let's consider the six situational styles to manage tensions involving teams.

The *visionary style* of leadership is practiced by leaders who like to paint the bigger picture and are goal-oriented. They communicate the vision to facilitate the alignment of the teams. This approach is good when you are leading an organization where a significant change is needed. A visionary leader is a great communicator with an unwavering belief in what she wants to accomplish.

This leadership style inspires those in an organization to commit themselves to the vision. To use this approach effectively, you need to be authentic, self-aware, and empathic. If your organization sees that you are merely paying lip service, it will backfire. You need to avoid projecting an overinflated view of yourself. New Zealand's Prime Minister Jacintha Ardern is an example of an inspirational leader. She is good at communicating her vision. She stayed authentic and kept New Zealand safe during the COVID-19 pandemic.

To be an effective visionary leader, use 360-degree feedback from time to time to evaluate how you are doing. Continue to improve your self-awareness and check your vision to make sure it remains current, and if not, tune it. Communicate frequently on how the organization is doing regarding the goals and continue to learn.

The *coaching style* of leadership is about the holistic development of team members. This type of leader empowers the team to become excellent. She is a changemaker and who can develop an organization to become a better version of itself.

Today, we understand a leader must act as a coach in the face of constant changes. The coaching style creates excellent results when the leader can identify her team member's individual goals, align them with the organizational goals, and provide development opportunities. The coaching leader appreciates the unique contribution of each team member and works to empower them. They foster this coaching mentality in all the managers in the organization.

There are different methods of coaching. In directive coaching, the leader directs the team, and it is effective when working with individuals who have limited skills and are seek direction. Another method is where the leader acts as a facilitator. She listens to the individuals, learns what would work, and then teaches them. They then collaborate to address the situation. Facilitative coaching works well with self-motivated teams who possess domain knowledge. I prefer to use a situational style of coaching, which requires you to assess both the situation and the individual being coached.

Satya Nadella, the CEO of Microsoft, is an excellent example of a coaching leader. He used situational coaching to move his fading company to a successful one. Nadella introduced several activities to cultivate the growth mindset of his employees. Under his leadership, Microsoft conducted hackathons and encouraged employees to work outside their regular responsibilities to develop themselves. He promoted projects that are considered "smart risks." These projects created new leaders. Nadella spends some of his precious time on a program called "Talent Talks."[6] This program identifies, cross-trains, and develops future leaders, supplementing the existing ones to develop high-potential employees.

For the coaching leadership style to be effective, the team members need to be invested in being coached. They must accept they need coaching. This approach works best when combined with visionary leadership.

The *democratic style* of leadership or participative leadership allows everyone's views to be heard. The leaders who use this approach make most decisions with consensus. Democratic leaders understand they don't have all the answers and work collaboratively with those they trust to solve problems. They believe in sharing ideas, keeping an open mind, and working to inspire trust.

A democratic leader promotes high empowerment among self-motivated team members. They encourage creativity and camaraderie. A team with this kind of leadership becomes adept at solving complex problems. There are some downsides to its use. Decision-making takes longer and all team members might not be happy with the results. It also doesn't work when a crisis happens, and you have to decide quickly. Tim Cook of Apple, former CEO Indra Nooyi of PepsiCo, and Eric Schmidt of Google are known as excellent democratic leaders.

A democratic leader is successful when all team members understand the organization's goals , and it is highly effective with competent teams. To make it work, you should have developed excellent communication, meeting management, and facilitation skills. Use this style when appropriate. Sometimes you should be comfortable deciding on your own.

The *affiliative style* consciously puts people above what needs to be done. A leader who uses this approach is a relationship builder. She is not afraid to be vulnerable in front of her team. She considers the welfare of the team in everything she does. When a task needs to be done, she cares not only about the deadline, but how well the team members work with each other in getting to the target.

This style can be highly effective when combined with coaching and visionary approaches. When organizational morale is low, the leader can use praise and helpfulness to build up the team's confidence. When used as the only one without combining other styles, poor performances could fester. It is also not effective in crises.

Early in my career, I focused only on results. The team members who thrived under my leadership were like me. As I progressed in my career, getting 360-degree feedback followed by leadership coaching helped me see my blind spots. I learned how to promote harmony among my team members and use the affiliative style when the situation warranted it. When I retired from the company I cofounded, this endorsement I received thrilled me:

> *Even in the most challenging situations, Shantha helped maintain the morale of the team and led the team in the most efficient manner. She made me and the team believe in ourselves, motivated us, and was a great supporter and leader. Her vision, passion, and leadership skills are something I will always look up to.*

If you are a leader who puts results above all else, pay more attention to your team members. Ask yourself what makes them tick and work with their strengths. Coach them to recognize and address their weaknesses. Make use of informal communication. Get close to the team members and listen carefully, and act on what you learned. Empower your team. If you find yourself ineffective with this leadership style, review the team members' performance and help them. Combine the style with others, such as visionary and coaching styles.

The *pacesetting style* of leadership is practiced by those who set high expectations for themselves and their followers. The leader with this style is intent on doing things faster and better. She will not tolerate poor performers and will quickly replace them. Burnouts among the team members are common under this type of leader. Yet this type of leadership can work under some conditions.

In my experience, highly motivated team members who are stellar performers thrive under this leadership. All I needed to do was to set the pace and have them run with it. I took care not to use this approach with all team members. That would have been a recipe for disaster. If you shy away from using it with your star performers, they may get bored and leave your team. You may be able to use this style with a select few on your team. But you should recognize when to ease up on your relentless drive, and you are highly knowledgeable about the capabilities of the team members. The key is to decide who can benefit from this approach and when.

The *coercive style* of leadership is one where the leader tells their subordinates what to do. She has a clear vision of the endgame and how to reach it, which is good in crises.

Leaders with this style rarely seek input from their teams, but are quick to provide feedback when things go wrong. Innovators don't thrive under them. This approach kills new ideas originating from the lower levels of the organizational pyramid and demoralizes the team. During stable times, this leadership style can lead to low morale and attrition of team members. It is most damaging to the climate of the organization. Leaders should use this approach only in extreme cases or with failing team members who need a shot in the arm.

Use Tensions to Learn and Grow

Leaders need to handle many opposing forces. Every decision has its pros and cons. You can manage leadership tensions by assessing the situation at hand and using a style that fits. You become better at leading with time, practice, and flexibility. Aspiring leaders would do well to develop their emotional intelligence to handle the tensions. Understand your dominant style and temper it as needed.

Practice

- Identify the leadership style you used in the recent past. Analyze each to see what you could have done differently. Next time you come across a similar situation, use what a situational leader might have done.
- Use the coaching style of leadership with your team. Learn how you can adapt it to your authentic way of leading. Explore how you can combine this with visionary leadership.

Balancing the Tensions—Questions to Ask Yourself

- What is my current leadership style?
- Where do I need development to be a well-rounded leader?
- If I am not using a coaching style of leading, what are the reasons?

Notes

1. Barry Miles, *Paul McCartney: Many Years from Now* (Holt Paperbacks, 1998).

2. Uri Friedman, "New Zealand's Prime Minister May Be the Most Effective Leader on the Planet," *The Atlantic*, April 19, 2020, accessed June 10, 2021, https://www.theatlantic.com/politics/ archive/2020/04/jacinda-ardern-new-zealand-leadership-corona- virus/610237/.
3. Tom Peters (Twitter handle: @tom_peters), accessed July 19, 2021, https://tompeters.com/.
4. Tom Peters' Tweets, accessed July 19, 2021, https://twitter.com/ tom_peters/status/1392165488436944896.
5. Daniel Goleman, *Leadership that Gets Results* (Harvard Business Review Press, 2017).
6. Larry Emond, "Microsoft CHRO: A Conversation about Succession Management," *Gallup*, 2018, accessed September 16, 2021, https://www.gallup.com/workplace/237113/microsoft-chro -conversation-succession-management.aspx.

Resources

Daniel Goleman, *Leadership That Gets Results* (Harvard Business Review Press, 2017).
Michael Bungay Stanier, *The Coaching Habit: Say Less, Ask More & Change the Way You Lead Forever* (Page Two, 2016).

CARE

4

Chapter 14

Let It Be

Everyone encounters stress, and leaders are no exception. Some amount of pressure is good for spurring us on to action. Business leaders deal with stress in many situations related to resources, economic conditions, and competition. We have seen these situations multiplied in today's complex world. The recent coronavirus pandemic took stress levels even higher. You can learn to handle stress by developing optimism, resiliency, and flexibility. Better sleep habits, exercise, and meditation are keys to building your stress tolerance and becoming the best leader you can be.

About the Song

The Beatles released "Let It Be" in March 1970. Shortly after that, McCartney announced his

DOI: 10.4324/9781003267546-18

departure from The Beatles. Paul got the idea for the song after he had a dream about his mother. This was during the time the relationship between the members of the band was strained beyond bearable. In the dream, his mother told him to let things be and everything will be alright.

Rolling Stone magazine ranked this song as 20th in its 500 greatest songs of all time.

Let It Be—Handling Stress

I choose how I react to stress.

"Let It Be" is one of my favorite Beatles' songs. It is also my anthem when I feel stressed.

I was leading several global software engineering teams in my 40s. The demands of my travels, work hours, and trying to be a super homemaker all contributed to my stress and manifested in my disease—diabetes—when I turned 50. If I knew then what I know now, I would have taken care of the stress in one of many ways. Mine is not an isolated example. In a study on stress,[1] 88% of leaders reported that work is a primary source of stress in their lives.

Impact of Stress

Merriam-Webster defines stress as "a state of mental tension and worry caused by problems in your life, work, etc." Stress is a natural human response in situations that put us under pressure. The right level of stress helps us with our achievements. Excessive stress becomes life-threatening. When you experience stress, your pulse quickens, blood pressure increases, you are tense, and your breathing becomes rapid. If the stress is short-lived, damage can be contained. However, prolonged periods of stress can lead to diseases, including mental breakdown.

All of us experience stress every day at work. Business leaders deal with resource shortages, employee conflicts, unhappy customers, stock prices (if you are a public company), pressures from investors, competition, technical shortcomings—the list goes on.

The COVID-19 pandemic subjected us to a lot of stress, some more than others. Many leaders felt helpless. The

American Psychological Association published a report on stress in January 2021.[2] They based it on an online Harris Poll survey from April 24 to May 4, 2020, which included 3013 adults age 18+ who live in the United States. This report showed seven in ten employed adults say work is a significant source of stress in their lives, which is also higher than the proportion of adults who cited this as a stressor in the 2019 survey. We don't know how many of these adults are in managerial or leadership roles. However, given that the employees look to leaders to help them, we can hypothesize it is in that range for the leaders too.

The pandemic brought a new way of working for many of us—working from home. We traded the commute for back-to-back online meetings. Parents needed to become responsible for their children's education. All this has created stress in our lives, besides the worry of contracting COVID-19.

Optimal Stress

Psychologists have been studying stress for a long time. In 1908, psychologists Robert Yerkes and John Dillingham Dodson conducted experiments on mice. They administered varying levels of electric shocks to them to observe their behavior in navigating a maze. While mild shocks propelled the mice to complete a maze, powerful shocks sent mice scurrying around all over the cage. They were not able to navigate the maze. This study resulted in the so-called Yerkes-Dodson Law that says peak performance and optimal stress relate to each other. You can explain how individuals perform in test-taking, public speaking, or sports using this law. With too much pressure, the test-taker cannot focus and fails the test. Speakers experiencing too much stress can become

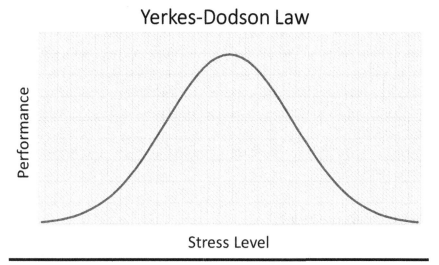

Figure 14.1   Yerkes-Dodson Law.

tongue-tied. In sports, a player might choke on a big game under high pressure.

We can express the Yerkes-Dodson Law as a bell-shape curve (Figure 14.1). Each of us is unique, and the stress tolerance differs from person to person. We characterize the curve to the left as stress that creates the impetus to perform. That force tells us to do whatever it takes to get a job done. When stress levels increase, we see a decline in performance after a certain level, and when the stress becomes too much, it can become unhealthy in various ways.

Types of Stress

The American Psychological Association classifies stress into three categories: acute, episodic acute, and chronic. We all experience acute stress in our lives. The upcoming town hall meeting with team members, a company board meeting, a deadline for a project, an upcoming test, a performance review, or even a health exam could create stress. Some of us experience these acute stresses repeatedly, named episodic acute stress, which might cause panic attacks, heartburns, and other problems. The third type is chronic stress. It stems from environmental, structural, or societal issues, such as poverty and racism.

Let us look at how we can manage the acute and episodic acute stresses.

Stress Management

In the *Authority Magazine* interview,[3] Michael Sachse of Dandelion Energy told a story when the interviewer asked about his principle behind handling business fluctuations.

It was a tale about a Taoist farmer and a runaway horse. All the villagers are sorry that the farmer lost the horse. But he says, "We'll see." The horse comes back to the farmer, bringing along four more horses. Now the villagers celebrate the farmer's good luck. The farmer's response? "We'll see." The farmer's son has the task of breaking horses, and while doing so, falls and breaks his leg. The villagers are full of sympathy for the farmer. "We'll see," is the farmer's response. Just then, the army comes and drafts all the healthy males in the village. However, because of his broken leg, they spare the farmer's son. Sachse says, running a business is not life and death. However, when you are going through troubles, it almost seems like it. When things are going well, you feel terrific. When you experience setbacks, you think the world is ending. In reality, what we experience at the moment may rarely play out that way.

Three important leadership characteristics can help reduce stress (Figure 14.2).

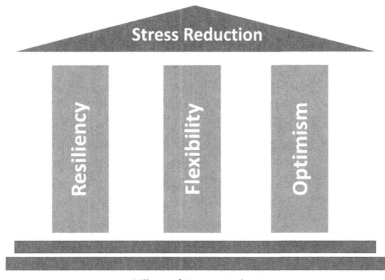

Pillars of Stress Reduction

Figure 14.2   Pillars of stress reduction.

Resiliency

One of these is resiliency. In an article,[4] writer Konnikova describes her discussions with George Bonanno. He is a clinical psychologist and head of the Loss, Trauma, and Emotion Lab at Columbia University's Teachers College. He has been studying resilience for a long time and has a theory about stress and resilience. Bonanno believes that we all possess the same fundamental response system for stress. A lot of us are good at using this response. But some of us use the system more efficiently and cope better under pressure. How you respond depends on how you perceive the stress-inducing event. If you consider it traumatic, you react one way. If you perceive the event as an opportunity to learn and to grow, you respond differently. Bonanno characterizes events as having "the potential" to be traumatic. Look at events that could become traumatic as learning opportunities to build resiliency and the ability to cope with stress.

Flexibility

Another characteristic that helps you deal with stress is flexibility. It helps you adapt your feelings to changing situations and environments. Leaders who can tolerate stress are flexible. They possess a mindset that allows them to bend and not break. They can adjust their behavior and emotional responses to deal with stressful situations. You can gain flexibility. Self-awareness is the starting point. Tasha Eurich discusses the findings from a large-scale study of close to 5000 participants in an article.[5] The study concluded that, to be truly self-aware, leaders must have both internal and external self-awareness. External self-awareness is about how others see you and is hard to know. You can achieve it if you are open and ask for feedback from those who care about you. Eurich also says that "what" questions are the hallmark of those with self-awareness. When you learn to see yourself clearly, you become flexible, and with flexibility comes the ability to cope with stress. In particular, you are aware of your stress triggers and your reaction to them. In a stressful situation, instead of asking "why me," ask "what can I do differently," which is an effective way to deal with stress.

Optimism

Optimism is the third pillar of characteristics that helps deal with stress. A study on finance-induced stress,[6] conducted in 2018 across 2,002 adult American participants, found that optimists were seven times more likely to experience less stress. Optimistic leaders look beyond the obstacles and feel hopeful, which can reduce stress.

How do you develop optimism? By observing yourself in situations where you use negativity, you can gradually get to optimism or positivity. For example, when someone mentions an idea, is your first reaction "not going to work?" Or, when you read an article, are you quick to pick out everything that is wrong with it, instead of understanding what is good? You can practice moving away from this extreme pessimism toward optimism by analyzing how you respond to others. Another way to develop optimism is to study those in your network who are optimistic and learn their behavior.

Foster a Positive Team Culture

Earlier in this chapter, we talked about optimal stress. A positive team culture will create an environment with optimal pressure. As a leader, your responsibility is to promote and grow such an environment. Encourage positive social connections in your team. You can extend your resilience and optimism to your team by leading your team with compassion. Encourage your team members to converse with you by being available to them. Lead with your head and your heart.[7]

Coping Mechanisms

We discussed self-awareness earlier, which is a critical component of emotional intelligence. Besides helping you become flexible, it can also help you with ways to cope with stress. Managing stress starts with understanding the cause. Your work, which is a top stress inducer, might be the reason. WebMD lists many other reasons for stress. For many, it is related to their finances. Others stress about health, relationships with family members, the death of a loved one, or life changes, such as switching jobs or moving to a new location. Once you identify the cause, the next step is to understand your reaction to it. Each of us deals with stress in our unique ways. Some of us tend to retreat within ourselves or get angry.

Others experience physical manifestations such as tiredness, having headaches, or being tense.

Next comes understanding how stress manifests in our behaviors. When I was young, I lived in my uncle's house for a short while. Every day, when my uncle returned from work, we learned to leave him alone until he was ready to interact with us. He wanted to be alone after a stressful day at work. Some might resort to unhealthy coping mechanisms, such as taking out their anger on their loved ones or turning to substance abuse, such as alcohol or drugs, or binge-eat.

By understanding how we behave, we can find coping mechanisms. A trained psychologist can help with these strategies when the stress is severe and is overtaking your life. Suppose you can identify what causes you stress, and you are confident you can handle it. In that case you should be able to craft coping mechanisms such as having a trusted friend to talk things over or getting involved in activities such as volunteering in the community or participating in sports. Stress is unavoidable when you are a leader. Be proactive in building a social support network that can help you manage stress. Work is known to be a primary cause of stress, so set boundaries for work-related activities. Instead of giving up vacations, take time off from work. Turn off all the gadgets that connect you to work and relax. When encountering leadership challenges that overwhelm you, turn to a trusted mentor or advisor to help find solutions. You can use a supportive peer network and delegate work to handle stress at work.

Laughter

Though science is yet to confirm it, laughter seems to help deal with health and stress. The article, "Laughter

Prescription,"[8] talks about cancer survivors who used laughter to cope with their situations. In this article, a cancer survivor spoke about how cancer made him experience anger and denial and feeling less human. Laughter made him open to ideas, people, and relationships. It made him more human than he thought before because of the illness.

Sleep

A *Harvard Business Review* article[9] asserts that there is a clear link between effective leadership and adequate sleep. There is also a connection between sleep and stress. When you are stressed, you can't sleep. When you don't get enough sleep, your tension builds up. It is a Catch-22 situation.

Experts suggest that there are things you can do to help you sleep when you are stressed. They include following a regular sleep schedule, a bedroom set up to be conducive to sleep with the right temperature and light, light meals consumed early in the evening, and moderate exercise early in the day. There are ways to manage your sleep, which then can reduce your stress.

Nutrition

Similar to the connection between sleep and stress, there is a two-way link between nutrition and stress.[10] While we need more clinical research on this topic, we seem to accept that good nutrition helps the brain deal with stress much better than foods void of nutrition, such as highly sweetened soft drinks and snacks. Pressure drives us to eat such foods, fueling more stress. Because of this, we consume lesser quantities of nutritious foods such as whole grains, fruits, and vegetables.

Population studies show that a healthy, balanced diet leads to better mental health.

Nature

A research was conducted in 2019[11] in England to understand the impact of exposure to nature involving close to 20,000 people. The study found that those who took part spent two hours per week in nature reported they were in good health and had higher psychological well-being than those who didn't do so at all. In Japan, "forest bathing" or "Shinrin-yoku" has been popular since the 1980s. Ecotherapy is to be in nature and use your senses of smell, hearing, sight, taste, and touch to experience nature. Several other studies say that being in a forest environment decreases the symptoms of stress and promotes emotional well-being, compared to being in a city environment.

Exercise

We understand the physical benefits of exercise well. Now, we know that it also has mental benefits. In 2011, 2013, and 2015, the Centers for Disease Control and Prevention conducted surveys to understand behavioral risk factors. A study[12] analyzed data from more than a million adults who took part in it. It looked at different parameters, including duration, type, and frequency of exercise. Those who exercised had fewer days of poor mental health compared to those who didn't. The effect was the largest with team sports, cycling, or aerobic exercises. Those who exercised three to five times a week for 45 minutes benefited the most. We understand exercising releases natural mood elevators by producing more endorphins in the brain. Activities such as simple breathing and yoga are also beneficial to mental health.

Mindfulness

Merriam-Webster defines mindfulness as follows:[13]

1: the quality or state of being mindful
2: the practice of maintaining a nonjudgmental state of heightened or complete awareness of one's thoughts, emotions, or experiences on a moment-to-moment basis

Studies support that mindfulness meditation helps reduce stress[14] and promotes overall physical and mental well-being. You can start with a class at a yoga center. Or you can try a mindfulness app available on your smartphone.[15]

Manage Your Stress—Let It Be

Resiliency, flexibility, and optimism are must-have leadership characteristics. These are also essential for dealing with stress. It would be helpful if you created a plan to enhance them as part of your personal development. Eat right, exercise, and get enough sleep. Develop coping skills by practicing mindfulness meditation. You can manage stress and be the best leader you can be.

Practice

■ Mindfulness meditation

Handling Stress—Questions to Ask Yourself

■ Do I know my stress triggers?
■ Do I exercise regularly?
■ Is there a support network I can rely on in times of stress?
■ What is my coping mechanism? Is that healthy? Can I tweak it?

Notes

1. Leading Effectively Staff, "What Drives Leadership Stress—And How to Deal," Center for Creative Leadership, December 9, 2020, accessed June 9, 2021, from https://www.ccl.org/articles/white-papers/stress-of-leadership/.
2. "Stress in America™ 2020," American Psychological Association, May 2020, accessed June 9, 2021, https://www.apa.org/news/press/releases/stress/2020/report.
3. Charlie Katz, "Michael Sachse of Dandelion Energy: How We Plan to Rebuild in the Post COVID Economy," *Authority Magazine*, September 8, 2020, accessed June 9, 2021, https://medium.com/authority-magazine/michael-sachse-of-dandelion-energy-how-we-plan-to-rebuild-in-the-post-covid-economy-acfced3851da.
4. Maria Konnikova, "How People Learn to Become Resilient," *NewYorker.com*, February 11, 2016, accessed June 10, 2021, https://www.newyorker.com/science/maria-konnikova/the-secret-formula-for-resilience.
5. Tasha Eurich, "What Self-Awareness Really Is (and How to Cultivate It)," *Harvard Business Review*, January 4, 2018, accessed June 9, 2021, https://hbr.org/2018/01/what-self-aware-ness-really-is-and-how-to-cultivate-it.
6. Michelle Gielan, "This Is What Optimists Can Teach You about Dealing with Stress," *Fast Company*, June 23, 2019, accessed June 9, 2021, https://www.fastcompany.com/90367693/how-optimism-helps-you-deal-with-stress.
7. More on this in Chapter 11, "All You Need is Love."
8. William B. Strean, "Laughter Prescription", *Canadian Family Physician*, Vol. 55, No. 10 (2009): 965–967, accessed June 9, 2021, https://www.researchgate.net/publication/26891756_Laughter_prescription.
9. Nick van Dam & Els van der Helm, "There is Proven Link between Effective Leadership and Getting Enough Sleep," *Harvard Business Review*, February 2016, accessed July 13, 2021, https://hbr.org/2016/02/theres-a-proven-link-between-effective-leadership-and-getting-enough-sleep.
10. Eric Graber, "Nutrition and Stress: A Two-Way Street," *American Society for Nutrition*, January 14, 2021, accessed July 13, 2021, https://nutrition.org/nutrition-and-stress-a-two-way-street/.

11. Mathew P. White, et al., "Spending at Least 120 Minutes a Week in Nature Is Associated with Good Health and Wellbeing," *Scientific Reports*, Vol. 9, No. 1 (2019), https://doi.org/10.1038/s41598-019-44097-3.
12. Referenced in "The Link between Exercise and Mental Health", UCLA Health, accessed September 11, 2021, https://connect.uclahealth.org/2018/10/17/the-link-between-exercise-and-mental-health/.
13. "Mindfulness," Merriam-Webster, accessed July 12, 2021, https://www.merriam-webster.com/dictionary/mindfulness.
14. "Mindfulness Meditation: A Research-Proven Way to Reduce Stress," American Psychological Association, accessed July 12, 2021, https://www.apa.org/topics/mindfulness/meditation.
15. Courtney E. Ackerman, "Top 14 Apps for Meditation and Mindfulness (+ Reviews)," *Positive Psychology.com*, May 24, 2021, accessed July 12, 2021, https://positivepsychology.com/mindfulness-apps/.

Resources

Look for a mindfulness meditation center focused on reducing stress in your town.
"Building your resilience," *American Psychological Association*, 2012, accessed July 12, 2021, https://www.apa.org/topics/resilience.

Chapter 15

The Inner Light

Enlightened leaders are aware the answers are within themselves. This chapter builds on this wisdom and explains the benefits of investing in personal development and leadership skills. In today's networked world, there are so many options for a leader to do this. A framework for lifelong learning based on people involved and processes to use can be helpful. As an aspiring leader, you can start with self-awareness development, find role models to emulate, and seek help from mentors. You can leverage your network to learn. A robust process with elements of planning, evaluation, and continuous refinement can be helpful in your activities to develop yourself.

About the Song

Released on March 15, 1968, "The Inner Light" was the B-side of "Lady Madonna." George Harrison

DOI: 10.4324/9781003267546-19   **215**

wrote the song and incorporated several Indian instruments into it. Recorded in Mumbai, India, the instrumental track featured sarod, shehnai, and pakhavaj. Several Indian musicians, including Aashish Khan, Hanuman Jadev, and Hariprasad Chaurasia, played on it. The song has the distinction of being the first Harrison composition on a Beatles' single.

Juan Mascaró,[1] a Sanskrit scholar, helped compose this song. Juan translated Bhagavad Gita, an ancient Hindu scripture, from Sanskrit to English, and his first book was *Lamps of Fire*, a collection of teachings from world religions. The Beatles Music History[2] website says Mascaró sent a copy of the *Lamps of Fire* to George in November 1967, with a suggestion that George incorporates in his song a few words of the Chinese philosophical text, "Tao Te Ching." He picked out the verse he wanted George to consider, verse 47, and George followed up, using the chapter title "The Inner Light" as his song's title.

The Inner Light—Importance of Lifelong Learning

Leadership and learning are indispensable to each other.

—John F. Kennedy[3]

Leaders who understand their strengths and weaknesses are self-aware. They also recognize the need to be lifelong learners.

In the constantly changing world, we can't afford to be standing still because we will end up comprehending less and less. When you study successful leaders' lives, self-learning stands out as one of their top priorities. They gain insights through reading, testing what they learn, and practicing. Their lifelong learning includes sharing and teaching others.

A Personal Narrative

I am proud to proclaim that I am a lifelong reader. I have loved reading for as long as I can remember, and I inherited this from my father. We used to tease him for reading even scraps of newspapers wrapped around the merchandise we bought. When I was young, I read a lot of books in my native language Tamil. When I visited relative's homes, I would carry a book, and once I arrived, I would disappear with my book in the attic. Over the years, what I read changed substantially. When I got married, I loved that my husband was also passionate about reading. We passed on this love of reading to our children. I firmly believe reading is a habit that promotes lifelong learning. Today's youngsters can explore so much material on every subject available to them on the internet.

My career growth resulted from my prioritization of learning. I am forever exploring topics of interest on internet blogs, articles, and forums. When I retired a few years ago, I started sharing what I learned broadly on various social media. I discovered and learned from what others shared, which became a virtuous cycle. I reflect on what I read before sharing, adding my points of view. Reflection must accompany reading.

When you read, you are collecting insights, but they don't persist until you express them in your own words. To crystallize your thoughts, you must write. As a leader, you need to

David Perell
@david_perell

When you write something new, your brain swirls all over the place.

You move in fits and starts, stumble, and circle back on yourself.

But eventually, the idea clicks and you find your way.

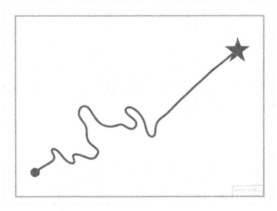

7:49 AM · Sep 17, 2021 · Twitter Web App

Figure 15.1   David Perell's tweet on writing.

communicate with different stakeholders, often through writing. Just with any other skill, you need practice to become good at it. Today, you can find many opportunities to practice your writing skills. You can write online blogs on topics of interest, or emails to your team members to thank them for a job well done. You can improve your writing by authoring professional articles in collaboration with a colleague. Write every chance you get.

David Perell, whose motto is "Write every day," is a writing teacher with a vast following on Twitter . His online course, "Write of Passage," helps those serious about writing online and promoting their thoughts. His tweet[4] (Figure 15.1) about what happens at the start of writing resonates with me.

Lifelong Learners

Pablo Casals was a famous cellist, composer, and conductor who lived during the early 20th century.[5] In 1963, President John F. Kennedy awarded him the Presidential Medal of Freedom. In his biography, written when he was 94 years old, he talked about aging. Casals said age is relative, and if you continue to work and learn and absorb knowledge, age does not mean getting old. Reporters asked him why he practiced for so many hours a day. Casals answered it was because he thought he was making progress. The hallmark of creative leaders is the mindset that you are never too old to learn.

Charles T. Munger is a famous American investor and vice chair of Berkshire Hathaway. Besides being a businessperson, he is an attorney, an architectural designer, and a philanthropist. We attribute the phrase "Latticework of Mental Models" to him. The mental models help you think better. Munger is a prominent proponent of reading and says wise people read all the time. He points to Warren Buffett, the chair and CEO of Berkshire Hathaway, as an example of a leader who is a voracious reader. Leaders get better when they read and learn every day. Charlie and Warren are excellent role models who do both, and they made their company the epitome of business success.

We hear so much about the reading habits of many successful business leaders. Steve Jobs showed great interest in the writings of William Blake, the British poet from the 18th century. Bill Gates reads three hours a day during his vacations. Elon Musk says he was "raised by books." Amazon's Jeff Bezos spent his childhood hours in a small library. The great political leader Winston Churchill's Nobel Prize was in literature.

John Maxwell, author, speaker, and pastor, shared his story of personal growth in an article.[6] In February 1974, John met Curt Kampmeier, President of the Kampmeier Consulting Group, over lunch. During the meal, John shared his dreams and aspirations with Curt. Deep in his heart, John felt those were out of his reach. Curt asked him if he had a plan, and John admitted he didn't. Curt told him personal development doesn't just happen and you need to plan for it. After explaining why John needed a plan, Curt offered to sell him a kit on personal development. However, John could not afford it as its cost was his entire month's salary. But his wife Margaret supported his aspirations. Together, they tightened their belts and saved, and in six months, John came up with enough money to buy the kit, which changed his life.

Framework for Lifelong Learning

Leadership growth happens with a personal development plan that promotes lifelong learning.

The first step in lifelong learning starts with a commitment to learning continuously. Give yourself time during the day just for education. The timebox technique[7] can help you with scheduling this as an item on your calendar. Understand your learning style. Many of us like to read books and articles. Others may learn better by watching videos or listening to audio. Be conscious of your learning style in finding the right resources. You may be interested in specific subjects and want to expand your understanding. You may be curious about others. Allow yourself time for serendipity, which makes learning fun.

Take personal responsibility for your learning. Executive education and leadership training are some ways you can learn, though not sufficient. Create a personal development plan. Figure 15.2 provides a framework to help you do it.

The framework has two parts. One of them is people-focused, and the other is process-focused. Leaders can use this framework to practice lifelong learning by putting them together and feeding each element from the other.

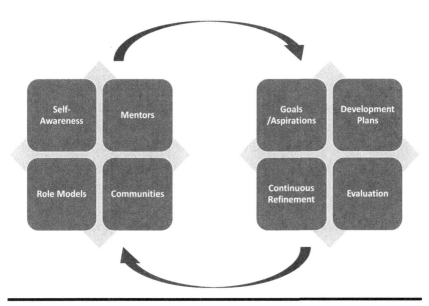

Figure 15.2   Personal development framework.

People Focused

Self-Awareness and Emotional Intelligence: Personal development requires that you recognize your strengths and weaknesses. You also need to have external self-awareness, how others see you. Research has shown that we become better when we see ourselves clearly and work on our shortcomings. Become a lifelong learner by understanding self-management. Self-management comprises self-control, adaptability, achievement orientation, and a positive outlook. Social awareness is the next component of emotional intelligence. This is about having empathy and being aware of those around you. This awareness nurtures your relationship with your colleagues, community, and family. By mastering relationship management, you can influence others. You can coach and mentor those you lead, manage conflicts, and inspire those in your organization. Self-awareness is essential to identify the gaps in your emotional intelligence and prepare for your personal development.

Role Models: Find a role model, someone you admire and would like to emulate. It could be in your immediate circle, in your family—the father, mother, older siblings, or someone at work. They may be in your community, or government, or world leadership. Strive to emulate their leadership qualities. Learn from them and personalize those qualities. Keep in mind that role models are not perfect. Your circumstances differ from those of role models. Your emotional intelligence can guide you in using what makes sense for you.

Mentors: Mentors can make a tremendous impact on a leader's self-development. Approach someone you admire and ask for their mentorship, but you must do your homework before you do. Does this person possess sufficient time to mentor you? What are your goals in approaching this person? What do you want to achieve in the mentoring relationship? In your lifelong learning, what aspect are you expecting to address? What deficiency in your knowledge do you want to overcome? Once you find a mentor willing to work with you, take responsibility for being a good mentee. Take care of the logistics involved in your meeting, setting agendas, and defining your learning objectives. Grow the mentor–mentee relationship with regularly scheduled meetings. You don't need to settle for just one mentor. You can develop a few mentors depending on your areas of interest. Your mentor is interested in knowing how you benefited from her sessions, so share your progress. Ask her if there is anything you can do to help her. A good mentoring relationship is reciprocal.

It may not be straightforward to get mentors, but you can find them. A 2019 study[8] found that 76% of people believe mentors are essential, but only 37% of people had mentors. Only 14% of mentor relationships started by asking someone to be their mentor; 61% of those relationships developed naturally. What this means is that you are likely to find mentors among those you already know. Today, social media is a great place to establish casual relationships, and you can expect to connect with someone on it. Such a relationship might become a mentoring engagement. I find social networks such as LinkedIn work well and I receive many requests for mentorship on this platform. You can search for mentors in professional associations. For example, the Institute of Electrical and Electronics Engineers (IEEE), Society of Women Engineers (SWE), and others are places where you can identify mentors. You may be able to get a referral for a mentor through a friend. Alumni associations are great places to find a mentor. When you have shared interests, you are bound to find those who like to mentor you.

Communities: Communities are your peers in the leadership journey. Connect with as many as you can. You can learn together, fuel each other's insights, and collectively make significant progress in self-development and lifelong learning.

You can get a lot from being part of communities. There are leadership forums where you take part by exchanging your thoughts with other participants. These forums host guest speakers who are experts on specific topics. For example, the Human Capital Institute's Annual Learning & Leadership Development Conference usually holds a three-day event, including presentations, interactive workshops, and networking opportunities. Videos are available to review post-conference if you cannot attend in person. In 2021, because of the pandemic, several leadership conferences went virtual.[9] Today, many communities are online. LinkedIn has groups interested in specific topics. The Executive Club[10] is one such group, meant for those who work at the executive levels of business, such as directors and vice presidents at medium- to large-sized companies. The communication within the group follows a Q & A format and members can post questions and get them answered by others. Facebook also has special interest groups where you can have positive learning experiences by browsing, reviewing, and choosing relevant content.

Process Focused

Goals/Aspirations: Learning cannot happen in a vacuum, so set goals for your learning. An overarching goal is to become a better leader. But you should set more specific targets, such as becoming a strategic thinker. Measure your progress as you make your journey in personal development. Your priorities change depending on the events that occur throughout your life. Be prepared to reset goals if necessary.

Development Plans: Whether you work with a mentor or learning community, create a development plan (Figure 15.3). The plan should identify specific areas for development, timeline, and means of accomplishing the goals you set for your learning.

For example, in continually learning to become a better leader, understand the history of leadership theories to get a perspective on what worked in the past and what trends are still applicable today. Read about prevailing trends in leadership since a style that worked in the 1950s may not work today. A sure way to keep progressing on your lifelong learning is to continue reading books and articles. You choose what to read and when to read it. Set aside time every day to do this. Besides understanding leadership theories, you will find material from your reading that you can use to engage with your community and prospective mentors. However, you cannot settle for reading about leadership. Without practice, what you read will remain theoretical. For example, skills such as giving feedback can be daunting. Practicing this in a low-risk situation can help.

Area of learning	By when?	How?
Public Speaking	End of June 2021	Toastmasters
Writing on a technical subject—4 articles	End of the year. One per quarter.	Create a website; post articles; share on social media
Writing on Leadership	End of the year. Two per year.	Post on the website; share on social media
Practice Gratitude	Continuous	Keep a journal and monitor if you are actively being grateful.

Figure 15.3   Learning goals.

To become a better communicator, start practicing public speaking. Besides improving your communication skills, it boosts your self-confidence, presents you with networking opportunities, and improves your thinking. As I mentioned earlier, reading and writing go together. Learn to write better. To become a humble leader, be consciously grateful and practice humility every chance you get.

Evaluate and Refine: Assess your development often, once in two weeks, or even once a week. Check how you are doing against the plan. Also, use the evaluation to refine your learning journey. Finally, the assessment should influence how you use community resources and mentors.

Learning and Social Networks

Harold Jarche[11] advises you to take personal responsibility for managing knowledge through social networks (Figure 15.4). He created a unique framework that comprehends the internet age. His framework advocates a continuous process of seeking–sensing–sharing as the way to be a lifelong learner. Seeking is about discovering insights through our networks. After searching and finding the knowledge we are interested in, we sign up to receive it. Sensing is about personalizing what we discover. It is about reflecting on what we learn

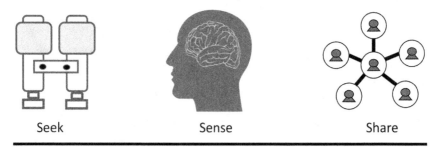

Seek   Sense   Share

Figure 15.4   The seek–sense–share framework.

and putting this into practice. Sharing involves spreading the wisdom we gain. You can do that by exchanging ideas, using peer-to-peer learning, and sharing experiences through various means, such as storytelling.

Be a Lifelong Learner

The world keeps changing. Every day, new insights are to be found. You don't want to be left behind. Commit yourself to a lifelong learning development plan. Learn from role models, mentors, and communities. Read voraciously. Develop, execute, evaluate, and refine a personal learning development plan.

Adam Grant[12] is an organizational psychologist and professor of management and psychology at Wharton. He is a best-selling author and has been Wharton's top-rated professor for seven consecutive years. I admire his motto, "Success is helping others succeed." His book *Give and Take*[13] made a profound impression on me, driving me to be a giver. I love the tweet[14] from him, as shown in Figure 15.5.

Learning enriches leadership. No matter how you do it, be a lifelong learner.

Adam Grant ✓
@AdamMGrant

Leaders who don't have time to read are leaders who don't make time to learn.

Leadership development depends not on your level of knowledge, but on your level of motivation to keep expanding your knowledge.

#WednesdayWisdom

Figure 15.5   Adam Grant's tweet on learning.

Practice

■ Find one area where you want to increase your understanding. Develop a personal learning framework and work on it.

Lifelong Learning—Questions to Ask Yourself

■ Do I have a mentor?
■ How strong is my knowledge network?
■ When was the last time I took part in a leadership conference?

Notes

1. "Juan Mascaró," Wikipedia, June 7, 2021, accessed September 2, 2021, https://en.wikipedia.org/wiki/Juan_Mascaró.
2. "The Inner Light," Beatles Music History: The In-Depth Story behind the Songs of The Beatles, accessed June 7, 2021, http://www.beatlesebooks.com/inner-light.
3. John F. Kennedy, Undelivered remarks prepared for the Trade Mart in Dallas, Texas, November 22, 1963. JFK was assassinated on the way to the Trade Mart, so he never actually delivered this speech or this line to an audience.
4. David Perell Tweet, accessed September 18, 2021, https://twitter.com/david_perell/status/1438877748848627712.
5. "Pablo Casals," Wikipedia, August 6, 2021, accessed August 24, 2021, https://en.wikipedia.org/wiki/Pablo_Casals
6. John C. Maxwell, "A Wonderful Christmas Gift," *johnmaxwell.com*, December 19, 2011, accessed June 9, 2021, https://www.johnmaxwell.com/blog/a-wonderful-christmas-gift/.
7. Matthias Orgler, "7 Secrets to Master Timeboxing," *Dreimannzelt Adventures*, April 21, 2016, accessed June 11, 2021, https://medium.com/dreimannzelt-adventures/7-secrets-to-master-timeboxing-66a744ea9175.

8. Olivet Nazarene University, "Study Explores Professional Mentor–Mentee Relationships in 2019," *Olivet.edu*, accessed June 9, 2021, https://online.olivet.edu/research-statistics-on-professional-mentors.
9. Human Capital Institute, HCI.org, accessed June 9, 2021, https://www.hci.org/conferences.
10. The Executive Club, LinkedIn, accessed June 9, 2021, https://www.linkedin.com/groups/2419859/.
11. "Harold Jarche," Jarche.com, accessed June 9, 2021, https://jarche.com/about/.
12. Adam Grant, accessed August 15, 2021, https://www.adamgrant.net/about/biography/.
13. Adam Grant, *Give and Take: Why Helping Others Drives Our Success* (Penguin Books, Kindle Edition, 2013).
14. Adam Grant Tweet, accessed September 18, 2021, https://twitter.com/AdamMGrant/status/1027185394096455680.

Resources

Carol S. Dweck, *Mindset: The New Psychology of Success* (Ballantine Books, 2007).

John C. Maxwell, *The 21 Irrefutable Laws of Leadership: Follow Them and People Will Follow You* (HarperCollins Leadership, 2007).

Chapter 16

When I'm Sixty-Four

While growing up, this song made me pause and think about what my life would be like when I get older. A leader who understands the conflicting priorities in her life and balances them has a better chance of getting to 64 with no regrets. There are times in our lives when we want to give more importance to what is going on in our personal lives, which is especially true when we have children who depend on us. Sometimes what happens at work takes priority. Learn how to juggle your time and attention and get to 64, a happy and satisfied leader.

About the Song

The Beatles recorded "When I'm Sixty-Four" in 1966 and released it in 1967 as part of the *Sgt. Pepper's Lonely Hearts Club Band* album. Apparently, this was one of the first songs written by McCartney at the age

DOI: 10.4324/9781003267546-20   **231**

of 15 or 16. The Beatles used to perform it in their early days. In 1966, The Beatles added some new lines, and the song made it into the album. Many Beatles' fans think it is too old-fashioned and not as good as the others on the album, but it has been my favorite through the years and a constant reminder of why family is important. The song is even more meaningful now that I am in my 70s and have grandchildren.

When I'm Sixty-Four—Balancing Family and Work

There is no work–life balance. Work is part of life.
Strive for a joyful life.

When you get to the age of 64, and look back on your life, would you say you are satisfied with how you lived it? We hear that if we live a balanced life, we would have every reason to say yes. The term work–life balance has been discussed so much in the media and has become a cliche. I am not a fan of this terminology. Work–life seems to imply that work is outside of life. I prefer to use the term work–family or work–home to talk about the balance in life (Figure 16.1). I define family as something unique to you. It may include just you, your friends, or a traditional family.

Figure 16.1   Home and work balance.

It Is Temporal

Can you find a balance between family and work? I say you can't always, not at a single point in time. You can, however, find a balance over your lifetime. During our life, we recognize periods when we give more importance to family than work and vice versa. In my case, I stopped working when my daughter was born. I became a stay-at-home mother until she was old enough to go to preschool and then started my graduate studies, which gave me all the flexibility I needed to spend time with my daughter. I finished my studies and took up a full-time job when she started elementary school. Many others like me choose to give importance to work or family depending on where they are in their life cycles.

Your family life has a tremendous influence on your performance as a leader. A leader who has wholehearted support from her family is very effective in her leadership role. A leader who cherishes her family gets tremendous support from her family.

Support Makes for a Balanced Life

In 1966, Sulochana, one of the pioneering women engineers I wrote about in my book *Roots and Wings*,[1] became the first woman chief engineer of civil designs at the Tamil Nadu Electricity Board (TNEB), India, a demanding job. It required her to travel to the field to do inspections. When I interviewed Sulochana's grown children for the book, her daughter Srilatha told me she still remembers her mother helping with homework after coming home from work. While helping her children, Sulochana would also attend to the paperwork she brought home from the office. Srilatha credits her mother with instilling in her excellent work ethic, the joy of working, and the can-do attitude that she hopes to pass on to her own two daughters. Sulochana's son Seshan is a technical leader and a women's advocacy engineer in the diversity efforts at his work. He credits his mother as his inspiration to become an engineer. Another son, Sathish, said watching her successful career felt like seeing a motivational speech come alive. All the children credited their father for standing behind their mother in her quest for leadership excellence.

Setting Boundaries

Susan Wojcicki is the CEO of YouTube and a mother of five children. In an interview with NBC show, *Today*,[2] she talks about why she always tries to be home to eat dinner with her children. She is home for dinner so that she has time to talk to her kids and catch up on what their days are like. Once they go to bed, Wojcicki is online, checking her emails. She has strived to retain more women with flexible work hours, special parking for expectant mothers, and a paid maternity leave of 18 weeks. Her article in the *Wall Street Journal*, "Paid Maternity Leave Is Good for Business,"[3] says when they increased paid leave at Google to 18 weeks, the rate at which new mothers left the job fell by 50%.

Zillow is an American online real estate platform. Its CEO Spencer Rascoff has been on the "Highest Rated CEOs" list of Glassdoor (the website where current and former employees review companies) several times. A Glassdoor interview says[4] he is home by 7 p.m. to be with his family. Unless he is on a business trip, you can find him at home spending time with his kids and dogs. He and other executives at the company set an example for a balanced life.

Clif Bar & Company, owned by family and employees, is an American company known for its healthy snacks. Its CEO Kevin Cleary takes time to coach his sons' sports teams.[5] He is very strict about when he sends out emails—no emails at night or on weekends. He doesn't want his employees to feel like they need to be working around the clock. When he gets home around 6:30, he leaves his phone in his home office. He pays attention to his kids and is fully engaged with them.

Many more leaders emphasize the need for a balance between work and home, coming from years of experience. You should pay attention to this critical advice.

Time between Family and Work

Leadership is time-consuming. But don't let that take time away from your family or self-care. Be deliberate in the balance of time you spend working and the time you spend with your family (Figure 16.2).

It isn't easy to achieve balance requiring conscious effort throughout your life. Many of us tie our identities to what we do at work. When we meet someone new, we usually introduce ourselves by announcing our professional title. It starts with that and permeates everything we do where we don't

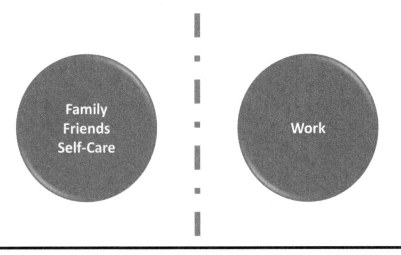

Figure 16.2 Work and family division.

identify ourselves beyond our work. We can do better by considering our entire selves.

In the BBC article, "Why It's Wrong to Look at Work–Life Balance as an Achievement,"[6] Bryan Lufkin discusses a study examining a group of 78 professionals to understand why some of them can distance themselves from their role at work and long hours of working. The input from the respondents with a better balance between their work and personal lives helped them identify five steps to achieve this. First, ask yourself if you should subscribe to the belief that you should focus on work all the time. This questioning helps you to identify issues of work-related stress and others and your feelings about them. Next, learn to label your emotions—sad, angry, etc. The third step is to use your emotions as leads to ask yourself if they were helpful and identify your priority. Next, consider different options to support your preference. The fifth and final step is to implement one or more of your options, defining a flexible work schedule for yourself and getting your team to support you in the decision.

Prioritize

Successful leaders understand what is important to them, both at work and at home. What is critical to one may not be important to another. For example, a business leader might consider financial rewards as vital to him in his work. Another leader might consider it essential to effect change. Many entrepreneurs start their businesses with this goal. Yet another leader might consider getting the respect of fellow human beings as a critical factor. Another might consider working on something she is passionate about as important. Similarly, from a home perspective, meaningful relationships with family members and friends, achieving a good standing in the community, or experiencing a well-lived life are essential for many of us.

Knowing what is important to you is the first step to a balanced life. What is your work priority, and what is your home priority? How do you reconcile these two when there is a conflict? Working closely with your partner at home can be of great help when you have children. When in doubt, asking your partner and then collectively deciding how to proceed is an excellent way to manage priorities. When you both share a vision of what is essential, you can expect a more balanced life. A workaholic, like me, benefited tremendously from hearing my husband stress the balance between home and work.

Get Support

Leaders don't need to go it alone. They can harness the support of colleagues at work, and family members, or friends at home. As I mentioned earlier, a leader like Sulochana counted on the help of her extended family and her husband to be a successful leader at work. When I led the product development team at Consilium, a Manufacturing Execution Systems (MES) company, we boasted of many preeminent semiconductor manufacturers as our customers. The locations of their fabrication facilities spanned the globe. I took many international trips to understand their needs better. I had a young child at home. My husband supported me and took care of the family while I traveled. The moral support provided by an understanding spouse goes a long way in meeting the demands at work. You can have a lot of give-and-take in the way families operate. When you and your spouse are in harmony, you can bounce ideas about work-related concerns off each other. Open communication and a shared vision for the family are critical to get good family support. Flexibility for both spouses at work is a must in today's demanding workplace.

Having support at work is equally important. You may need to deliver a major presentation. A key customer wants a meeting to discuss product features. A crisis demands your attention. You want to meet with a mentor who is your sounding board. When your demands at home are competing for your time, understanding colleagues can help you handle the needs at work. At Retail Solutions, the company I cofounded, where I held the post of Chief Development Officer, a crisis required traveling to another location. An equally important event was taking place at home—my daughter was delivering twins, and we had planned on my support months earlier. At work, my cofounders understood my priority—to be with my daughter. The VP of engineering who reported to me stepped up and took on the responsibility of dealing with the crisis with the help of others in the team. I took part remotely and provided direction.

It is vital to develop relationships and build your support network before you need any help. Relationships take time to develop. The best time to start is when you have nothing to gain from it. If you take a genuine interest in your peers and your team members, they will reciprocate, and in time, you will have a robust support system.

Manage Your Time

You can be strategic in how you spend your time at work and home. Today, when most parents work outside the home, they need to manage their time wisely between work and home.

If your team at work is empowered, you can trust them to do the day-to-day activities. Use your time on tasks of strategic nature where you can add value. Micromanaging is a time sapper. Avoid it. Prioritize the demands on your time with the help of techniques such as timeboxing. Use your calendar, not just for your meetings at work, but for personal activities that require your undivided attention.

At home, tasks that consume time can vary from the mundane—shopping, cleaning the house, cooking—and more important ones, such as spending time with your children. These activities are not equally important or strategic. You can get help with house cleaning from a cleaning service. When the children are older, they can take on some chores, and you can lower the level of service you get. Many services are available today for shopping and delivering goods. Avail of these services and spend the time saved with your children. You may not enjoy cooking. Takeout meals may be an option for you to save time. Others may enjoy cooking. They can turn this activity into a family event, each one cooking and sharing a dish. You can get logistics and household support from your support network—for example, carpooling for school or activities. However, if the activities include a performance or an important game, you would want to attend those. Use the time you save from the mundane activities to spend time with your children reading together, playing intellectually stimulating games, or sports that you both enjoy, walking or biking. More importantly, use the time to be available to them, listening to them when they experience setbacks or need your guidance regarding their future.

When children are older, many parents experience the "empty nest" syndrome. You miss them, but this is the most opportunistic time to indulge in things you skipped before. Pursue a second degree, or take up that hobby you always wanted to.

Time Away from Home

Work-related travel poses a problem because you are separated from those at home physically. However, today's technology provides us with many means to communicate. Choose how much you want to travel depending on the reason. If a meeting can be over the internet, you don't need to spend your precious time traveling. The COVID-19 pandemic created a situation where many of us were forced to work from home. Travel came to a standstill because of restrictions on movements across countries. Yet we continued to transact business made possible by tools such as Zoom, Teams, and WebEx. These tools help you stay connected with your family when you are away from home attending business. Conversely, they can help you conduct business when you choose not to travel for work.

Separation from the family is not always physical. Someone could be physically present but emotionally unavailable. Think about ways in which you can be accessible to your family by working on your approachability.

A Balanced Life

Our priorities change over our lives. The key to living a balanced life is to know what counts when. You cannot have a balance between work and home life at every point in time. However, you can live to 64 and be happy with your life. The key is to juggle your priorities and manage your time. Be strategic about how you spend it, using modern productivity tools to help you. I am at the point in life where my priorities are my grandchildren, lifelong learning, and giving back to society. Many of you may like to travel with your spouse to places on your bucket list or relax on a beach reading your favorite book. Some of you may want to write a memoir or start a second career. Whatever you aim for, if you live a balanced life, you can be satisfied when you are 64.

Practice

- Next time you have to travel for work, be deliberate about asking if you can avoid it.
- Learn to timebox your calendar with not just work activities, but activities with your family. Keep the commitments you make.

Balancing Family and Work—Questions to Ask Yourself

- Do I have interest outside work?
- Am I spending enough time with my children or friends?
- How well do I take care of my physical and mental well-being?

Notes

1. Shantha Mohan, *Roots and Wings: Inspiring Stories of Indian Women in Engineering* (Notion Press, 2018).
2. "YouTube CEO Susan Wojcicki on Balancing Work and Family," *Today*, December 5, 2014, accessed June 11, 2021, https://youtu .be/vZ0yrlVebvA.
3. Susan Wojcicki, "Paid Maternity Leave Is Good for Business," *Wall Street Journal*, December 16, 2014, accessed June 11, 2021, https://online.wsj.com/articles/susan-wojcicki-paid-maternity -leave-is-good-for-business-1418773756.
4. Emily Moore, "Why Zillow Group CEO Spencer Rascoff Is Home by 7 P.M. Almost Every Night," *Glassdoor*, June 21, 2017, accessed June 11, 2021, https://www.glassdoor.com/blog/zillow -group-spencer-rascoff-interview/.
5. Susanna Kim & Michael Rothman, "The C-Suite Insider: Clif Bar CEO Kevin Cleary Pays Workers to Exercise 2.5 Hours a Week," *ABC News*, October 28, 2014, accessed June 11, 2021, https:// abcnews.go.com/Business/suite-insider-clif-bar-ceo-kevin-cleary -pays/story?id=26489345.

6. Bryan Lufkin, "Why It's Wrong to Look at Work–Life Balance as an Achievement," *BBC Worklife*, March 1, 2021, accessed June 11, 2021, https://www.bbc.com/worklife/article/20210302-why -work-life-balance-is-not-an-achievement.

Resources

Bill Burnett & Dave Evans, *Designing Your Life: How to Build a Well-Lived, Joyful Life* (Knopf, 2016).
Matthew Kelly, *Off Balance: Getting Beyond the Work–Life Balance Myth to Personal and Professional Satisfaction* (Blue Sparrow, 2015).

The End—Take Charge!

Here we are, at the end of the book, and what is more appropriate than to conclude with The Beatles song "The End"[1]—a medley recorded by The Beatles when they were winding down their career.

The complexities of today's world demand that a leader harness all the power of her team to solve problems and achieve goals. When you get promoted to be a manager, you cannot meet the demands of that position if you don't have any management training. Many MBA programs fall short of teaching so-called soft skills. When I first became a manager, I had no compass to show me how to lead my team, except for my inner one. I learned by observing and experimenting. With the insights I am giving you in this book, you need not depend on only watching and winging it. Some of you may already be well into your leadership journey. While the content may not be all new to you, I hope you discover something new in how I organized and presented it.

If you are an aspiring leader, there is enough knowledge in this book to put things immediately into practice and explore more on your own with the resources provided. The chapters on various leadership attributes give you the basic foundation. They will not only be helpful throughout your leadership journey, but will also serve you well in your life. These are fundamental to being an illustrious leader.

DOI: 10.4324/9781003267546-21

Five chapters describe tools you will often use every day. The lessons on communication, negotiation, being available, empowering your team, and leading with love and compassion are like the blades of a Swiss knife, where each blade is a specific skill.

Chapters on mastering the use of intuition and managing leadership tensions are sure to serve you well as you grow in your role as a leader. I hope you can take away meaningful insights from the final chapters on handling stress, lifelong learning, and balancing work and family.

For each chapter, I am giving you a mantra from the music of The Beatles. Each of the titles represents the specific leadership lesson irrespective of the lyrics. One of my mentees with whom I shared Chapter 8, "We Can Work It Out," told me she was listening to the song in a loop when she was concerned about resolving a conflict with her business partner. I am hopeful you feel that way about all the chapters.

You cannot become a better leader by just reading about it. Get out and practice. I have given you some practice tips. Each of your situations is different. I hope you will take the suggestions as examples of what might be possible in your case and create your own—Think for Yourself. Own your leadership journey. Take charge.

Note

1 "The End (Beatles song)," Wikipedia, accessed October 9, 2021, https://en.wikipedia.org/wiki/The_End_(Beatles_song).

Index

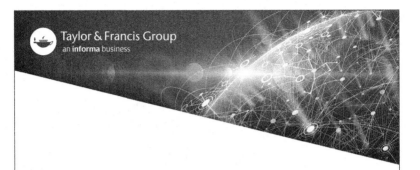